British WARSHIPS Since 1945

Part 4

MINESWEEPERS

MW01155891

M295

by Jack Worth

Edited by Mike Critchley

£3.75

MINESWEEPING
SQUADRON LOCATIONS

1st Minehunting Squadron	1.10.62 to 1966. Port Edgar.
1st MCMS	1-66 to 1984. Formed to combine the function of the 1st Minehunting, 2nd & 5th Minesweeping Squadrons. Port Edgar.
2nd MSS	1,10.62 to 1966. Port Edgar.
2nd MCMS	1972-1984. Portsmouth.
3rd MSS	1.10.62 to 1966 Portland.
3rd MCMS	1966 to 1980. Portland. 1.1.84. Reformed at Rosyth.
5th MSS	1.10.62 to 1965. Portsmouth (Originally Vernon Squadron).
6th MSS	1.10.62 to 1.6.73. Far East.
7th MSS	1.10.62 to 1969. Mediterranean.
8th MSS	1.10.62 to 1967. Hong Kong.
9th MSS	1.10.62 to 1971. Middle East.
10th MCMS	1.10.62 to 1984. RNR Divisions.
11th MSS	1965 to 1966. Far East. 1982 Falkland Islands.
50th MSS	1955 to 1958. Port Edgar became 3rd MSS. 1.10.62.
51st MSS	1956 to 1962. Port Edgar became 1st MSS 1.10.62.
100th MSS	1957-58. Portsmouth. 1958-62, Port Edgar, became 2nd MSS. 1.10.62.
101st MSS	—1962 became 10th MCMS 1.10.62.
104th MSS	1954/56 Harwich. 1956/59 Med. 1959/62 Far East became 6th MSS 1.10.62.
105th MSS.	1956 Harwich.
108th MSS	1955/62 Mediterranean. Became 7th MSS 1.10.62.
120th MSS	1958/62 Hong Kong, became 8th MSS 1.10.62.
232nd MSS	1954/1956 Harwich.
Vernon Squadron	1956-1962. Originally M/S Training Squadron. Became 5th MSS 1.10.62.
6th Patrol Craft Squadron	1973/83 then renamed—Hong Kong Squadron.

———————————————

Acknowledgements

Without the assistance given by John Robbie of Glasgow, Jack Williams of Blackpool, and Paul Melton of the Naval Historical Branch MOD(N), the research for this book would have been even more difficult that it turned out to be!

Their help is greatly appreciated.

Photographs

We are grateful to the following for the use of their photographs in this book:

Dr Ian Buxton	Sid Goodman Esq.
Fleet Photographic Unit	RNAS Culdrose
Maritime Photo Library	RAF St. Mawgan
Western Morning News Ltd.	Wright & Logan Ltd.

MINESWEEPERS/MINEHUNTERS

A BRIEF HISTORY

Whilst the content of this book only covers minesweepers since World War 2—the history of these ships, that have had a vital—but unsung—role is given below.

In 1907 the Commander-in-Chief Home Fleet, Lord Charles Beresford, advocated the use of trawlers to sweep mines, since fishermen were experienced in the use of trawls. The Admiralty hired two trawlers and used them as experimental ships. This was so encouraging that a "Trawler Section" of the Royal Naval Reserve was formed.

At the outbreak of World War I in 1914, German minelayers were soon at work. The only regular Royal Navy minesweepers were six old converted torpedo gunboats of about 800 tons.

One-hundred trawlers were rapidly fitted out as minesweepers and joined the Reserve. The Admiralty also requisitioned holiday paddle steamers, as they had a shallow draught and were considered less vulnerable when sweeping minefields.

In June 1917, these minesweepers harvested some 500 mines but lost, on average, one minesweeper a day!

By 1918, thirty-two new 15 knot paddle minesweepers had been built. In addition 400 new trawlers were constructed. Twenty-six 'Hunt' Class Minesweepers were built during 1917-19, these coal burning minesweepers, or 'Smokey Joes' as they were known, made up half the Royal Navy's establishment of Fleet Minesweepers. They were built as a result of the shortcomings of the paddle minesweepers. The 'Hunt' class were designed to work in shallow waters with a speed, when sweeping, of about 12 knots.

During the war, 214 British minesweepers had been sunk, but there were still some 1,000 stationed at various ports at home and abroad at the end of the war; for them the war was far from over. The International Mine Clearance Committee asked the Royal Navy to help sweep an area of some 40,000 square miles.

The United Kingdom was one of 26 countries allocated with this task and by the end of November, 1919 had completed this operation, having swept over 23,000 mines.

On completion of the mine clearance programme, minesweeping forces were reduced and a number of former fishing trawlers were returned to their owners. Many Fleet Minesweepers were sold or broken up and the remainder placed in reserve.

The Royal Navy were prepared for any future mining of British waters by maintaining a flotilla of fleet minesweepers for training and the development of minesweeping techniques. This flotilla became the 1st Minesweeping Flotilla and three further trawlers were added for the training of men of the trawler section of the R.N.R. renamed the Royal Naval Patrol Service.

In 1933, the first four of the new 17 knot 'Halcyon' class of Fleet Minesweepers were laid down and 17 more were built during the 1930's. They were fitted with Asdic for A/S patrols and were used more for escort work than minesweeping.

The 'Halcyon' class was the basic design for all new Fleet Minesweepers built after them. When World War II broke out in August 1939, the Royal Navy, although short of minesweepers and men, had a sound nucleus of both on which to build. A number of trawlers were brought into use and new vessels ordered. Fish holds became mess decks and trawls were exchanged for mine sweeping gear.

The trawlers formed the Royal Naval Patrol Service based at Lowestoft, which was named H.M.S. 'Europa' in 1940. Initially these ships were manned by Skippers, Mates and the men of the R.N.R. (except for communication ratings). Later, the crews were to be fishermen, tugmen and lightermen.

In the official language of the Admiralty—these ships earned the nickname of 'Harry Tate's Navy', after the famous comedian of the 1920's and 30's. They even had their own badge, which was silver, and about the size of an old shilling. It took the form of a shield which showed a sinking shark transfixed by a marline spike, (representing the anti-submarine service) against a background of a fishing net containing two trapped mines (the minesweepers), the whole surrounded by a rope, with two fishermen's bends, topped by the Naval Crown. Below was a scroll bearing the letter 'M/S—A/S'.

Paddle steamers were once again brought into service as minesweepers, such ships as 'MEDWAY QUEEN', 'THAMES QUEEN' and 'GLEN AVON', all serving as such.

Destroyers of the 'A'—'I' classes were also equipped to operate sweeps ahead of the fleet.

The Director of Minesweeping put his faith in the paravane and the Oropesa sweep; the latter was a method used in the First World War for sweeping moored contact mines. A flotilla of minesweepers steaming in echelon each streamed one serrated sweep wire on one or the other quarter, (sometimes on both), each one overlapping the next astern. A kite kept each sweep wire at the required depth; a similar device, called an otter pulled the wire out on the required quarter.

The Admiralty learned that the Germans were using magnetic mines laid by Submarines. These mines were sown on the sea bed in shallow water, and were detonated by a magnetic needle activated by the ship's steel hull passing over it. Wire sweeps and paravanes were useless against the magnetic mine. The mine experimental department improvised with various possible methods, all based on the principal of towing electro-magnetics by minesweepers. They towed two electric cables on the surface, one of 750, the other 175 yards and passed an electric current down them. This produced a magnetic field of sufficient strength to explode the mines, and with minesweepers working in pairs, a wide area could be swept without difficulty. This electric sweep was known as the "Double L" sweep.

The Germans then introduced the acoustic mine which was activated by the sound of the ship's machinery passing over it.

British mine countermeasure developed was the acoustic hammer, a device streamed by a minesweeper to produce a false trail of noise, and the explosive sweep, which destroyed an acoustic mine by controlled explosions made under water.

The construction of minesweepers was increased to keep pace with the ever increasing use of the mine. Large numbers of small wooden 200 ton motor minesweepers were built to sweep shallow waters of harbour approaches.

Twenty-three 'Hunt' class fleet minesweepers supplemented the twenty-one 'Halcyons' and twenty ships of the new 'Bangor' class were under construction during World War II.

More than one hundred 'Bangor' class were built between 1940 and 1942, forty-five in British Yards, sixty in Canada, four in India two in Hong Kong and two at Taikoo. They were the first of a new class of fleet 'sweeper to be built for the Royal Navy. They were smaller than the 'Halcyon' and 'Hunt' class. These ships were designed, pre-war, for coastal minesweeping of moored mines but at the outbreak of the War they were modified and the building programme accelerated: They were fitted with additional equipment and armament to help meet the shortage of escort vessels. Named after British Ports they swept in home waters, and more distant waters of the Atlantic and Arctic oceans.

The 'Bangor' class were very useful Oropesa 'sweepers and carried out excellent work in this role, but, when influence sweeping became a necessity, their cramped decks emphasized the need for a larger type of minesweeper.

The new construction of minesweepers was increased to keep pace with the German mine offensive and the paddle 'sweepers were taken off minesweeping tasks as more new Fleet Minesweepers were commissioned.

Most efficient of all the wartime British Fleet sweepers were the 'Algerine' class, they were built between 1942 and 1945, armed with a 4 inch gun, four double oerlikon cannon and depth charges, and were generally designed to cope with the varied demands of magnetic, contact and acoustic minesweeping. They were however frequently used as Escort vessels.

Of the 110 ships built, 48 were built in British Yards and 62 in Canada.

When the war ended and all mine clearance operations concluded, the trawlers returned to their fishing grounds and the paddle steamers to their holidaymakers. The Fleet minesweepers were scrapped or sold, with the exception of the majority of the 'Algerine' class, these were retained for a number of years, but were gradually retired so that by 1965 there were no large minesweepers in the Royal Navy.

On 17th March, 1953, H.M.S. 'CONISTON', the first of a new class of coastal minesweeper was completed. These ships were built between 1953 and 1960 to meet the threat posed by modern mines. Experience gained in the Korean war showed that existing fleet minesweepers were too vulnerable. They were equipped to deal with contact, magnetic or acoustic mines. To protect these ships from the magnetic and acoustic influences of modern mines they were specially built of non-ferrous materials. The hulls were built of double mahogany and the superstructure of aluminium alloy and all other materials of the lowest possible magnetic content. They were protected from pressure mines as far as possible by their low displacement and the threat of moored mines was greatly reduced by their shallow draught.

To counter damage caused by marine parasites, some of the later ships were fitted with half inch protective wood and nylon sheathing on the outer shell below the water line.

These ships were to have been named after insects, and the first ships were allocated the following names, present names enclosed in parenthesis:

RED APHIS ('AMERTON'), BLUE APHIS ('APPLETON'), GREEN APHIS ('BEACH-AMPTON'), GOLDEN APHIS ('BEVINGTON') and so on.

In 1952 these names were dropped and numbers substituted, in 1953 they were named after villages in the United Kingdom ending in 'ton'.

The original squadron of 'ton' class was the 104th and is thought to have commissioned in about 1954. The squadron consisting of:— ALCASTON, (S.O.), APPLETON, BEVINGTON, BOULSTON, BRINTON, BURNASTON, CONISTON and EDDERTON.

An unknown CMS during Indonesian Confrontations.

During 1956, the 104th and the newly formed 108th joined the Mediterranean Fleet, with increasing numbers of minesweepers arriving from their builders, additional squadrons were formed, these were the 101st (later to become the VERNON Squadron), consisting of BEACHAMPTON, CAUNTON, GAVINTON and LALESTON.

By 1956 new Squadrons commissioned the 105th; APPLETON, BLAXTON, EDDERTON and UPTON, the 108th; SEFTON, DUFTON, FENTON, HICKLETON, HEXTON, LEVERTON, RODINGTON, FLORISTON, ALDINGTON, ESSINGTON,

KILDARTON, PENSTON, SHAVINGTON and DILSTON.

In home waters, the 104th (U.K.) CLARBESTON, the 105th; HIGHBURTON and ILMINGTON. The 50th based at H.M.S. LOCHINVAR, DALSWINTON and a number of Inshore minesweepers. The Reserve Fleet at Chatham included BURNASTON, BRINTON, CALTON, INVERMORISTON and TARLTON. A large number of mine-sweepers were also in reserve at Hythe, which included FISKERTON, LULLINGTON and MARYTON.

Since 1957, some Ton Class were converted to minehunters, the first—H.M.S. SHOULTON—was converted at Thornycrofts Yard, Woolston, and were regarded as among the finest of their type in the world. Equipped with sonar, they were able to locate and classify any mine-like object on the sea bed with an accuracy and range previously impossible.

At about the time that the 'ton' class were being built, a similar large number of in-shore minesweepers were being built, these were the 'Ley' and 'Ham' classes, built of wood or composite non-magnetic materials, designed to operate in shallow waters of rivers and estuaries.

Their construction was prompted by the 'Cold War' of the 1950's and as the situation thawed, many were laid up on completion without ever being commissioned. Others, after a short period of active service were laid up or sold to foreign navies. They were far from comfortable seaboats in open waters!

H.M.S. 'WILTON', the first G.R.P. Warship built for the Royal Navy was launched on 18th January, 1972, and completed on 12th June, 1973. Most of her equipment including the main engines were originally fitted in H.M.S. 'DERRITON' and were reconditioned by Vosper Thornycroft as part of the Ministry of Defence contract before installation. She was an experimental prototype and not the first of a new class for the Royal Navy.

The life of the present 'Ton' class minesweeper/hunters has been extended far longer than was intended when they were built in the 1950's. Having been used for the widest variety of work they have paid for themselves many times over—they are now (1984) proving expensive to keep operational.

The first of a new class, the Hunt's H.M.S. 'BRECON' has cost about £25 million compared to less than £900,000 for each of the existing vessels.

'BRECON' was ordered in April, 1975 the lead yard services were provided by Vosper Thornycroft (Woolston) who built the lead ship.

The new class is somewhat larger than the existing 'Ton' class. They are also the largest ships in the world to be built of G.R.P.

In order to come within the title of this book the careers of a number of ships have had to be deleted from the text.

After an active war-time career they saw no further service.

HUNT CLASS

Displacement:	710 tons (Tedworth 675 Tons)
Dimensions:	220 (pp) 231 (oa) x 28½ (Tedworth 28 x 7½)
Armament:	1 - 4", 1 - 3" AA.
Complement:	73

Name	Completed	Builders
ABERDARE	3.10.18	Ailsa, Troon.
ALBURY	17. 2.19	Ailsa, Troon.
ALRESFORD	26. 5.19	Ailsa, Troon.
BAGSHOT	1. 5.19	Allen, Ardrossan.
DERBY (ex Dawlish)	9.18	Clyde Shipbuilders.
FAREHAM	1. 9.18	Dunlop Bremner.
FLINDERS (ex Radley)	31.10.19	Lobnitz.
FORD (ex Fleetwood)	12.18	Dunlop Bremner.
* GOOLE (ex Bridlington)		Ayrshire Dockyard Co.
HARROW	23.10.18	Eltringhams, South Shields.
KELLETT (ex Uppingham)	13. 6.19	Simons, Renfrew.
LYDD	18.12.19	Fairfield, Govan.
PANGBOURNE (ex Padstow)	8. 5.18	Lobnitz, Renfrew.
ROSS (ex Ramsay)	29. 8.19	Lobnitz, Renfrew.
SALTASH	31.10.18	Murdoch & Murray, Yarrow.
SALTBURN	31.12.18	Murdoch & Murray, Yarrow.
SELKIRK	17. 3.19	Murdoch & Murray, Yarrow.
SUTTON (ex Salcombe)	23. 8.18	McMillan, Yarrow.
TEDWORTH	26. 6.17	Simons, Renfrew.

* GOOLE was laid up incomplete & in Nov. 62 was towed to Liverpool for BU.

HMS Lydd

7

HUNT CLASS — notes

Name	Date	Notes
ABERDARE	45-47	Harbour Service Malta.
	13. 3.47	Sold to Dohmen & Habets, Belgium for Mercantile use.
ALBURY	1.45-3.47	Reserve Fleet at Falmouth.
	13. 3.47	Sold to Dohmen & Habets, Belgium for Mercantile use.
ALRESFORD	1.45-3.47	Reserve Fleet Milford Haven.
	13. 3.47	Sold to Dohmen & Habets, Belgium for Mercantile use.
BAGSHOT	1. 4.45	Renamed Medway II as accommodation ship for submarines.
	28. 2.46	Reverted to BAGSHOT.
	1949	Sold for Mercantile service..
	1. 9.51	Mined under tow off Corfu and sunk.
DERBY	8.44-7.46	Laid up at Gibraltar.
	31. 7.46	Sold to G. McGrail, Gibraltar. BU in Spain.
FAREHAM	10.45 to	
	12.46	Accommodation ship for small craft at Malta.
	16.12.46	Paid off for towing to Plymouth.
	24. 8.48	Sold for BU by Ward at Hayle.
HARROW	10.44 to	
	7.47	In reserve at Malta.
	8.47	Sold J. Dacoutios, Malta for BU.
LYDD	Jan. 45	4th Flotilla (Plymouth).
	4/45-47	Reserve Fleet Milford Haven.
	13. 3.47	Sold in Belgium for Mercantile use.
PANGBOURNE	2.45-3.45	Reserve Fleet at Milford Haven.
	1.46	For disposal.
	13. 3.47	Sold to Dohmen & Habets, Belgium.
ROSS	1.45-3.47	Reserve Fleet, Milford Haven.
	13. 3.47	Sold to Dohmen & Habets, Belgium.
SALTASH	1.45-3.47	Reserve Fleet at Falmouth.
	13. 3.47	Sold to Dohmen & Habets, Belgium.
SALTBURN	26.10.45	Extensive Damage in Solent. Beyond economical repair.
	20.11.45	Paid Off.
	16.11.46	BU Gifford, Bude.
SELKIRK	1.45-9.48	Reserve Fleet, Milford Haven.
	17.5.47	Sold to Dohmen & Habets, Belgium.
	10.48	BU.
SUTTON	12.44 to	
	7.47	Reserve Fleet at Falmouth.
	7.47	Sold to Dohmen & Habets, Belgium.
TEDWORTH	1. 6.45	In collision with 'ROCHESTER'.
	11.46	Sold and BU by Ward of Hayle.

HALCYON CLASS

Twenty-one ships of this class were built, the last appearing just prior to the outbreak of World War Two in 1939. During the war many modifications were made to them which included new sweeps and AA weapons.

Displacement:	815 to 1370 tons.
Dimensions:	230' (pp) 245' (oa) x 33½' x 8'
Armament:	Varied 1 - 4", 1 - 4" AA., 2 - 4" AA (2 x 1)
	4 - 0.5" AA. (1 x 4)
Complement:	80.

Name	Completed	Builders
FRANKLIN	17. 8.38	Thornycroft, Ailsa.
GLEANER	30. 3.38	Central Marine, Grays.
HALCYON	18. 4.34	J. Brown.
HARRIER	9.11.34	Thornycroft.
HAZARD	24.11.37	Central Marine, Grays.
JASON	9. 6.38	Thornycroft, Ailsa.
SALAMANDER	18. 7.36	White, Cowes.
SCOTT	13. 2.39	Parsons, Caledon.
SEAGULL	21. 7.38	Richardson Westgarth, Devonport.
SHARPSHOOTER	16.12.37	Devonport Dockyard
SPEEDY	7. 4.39	White, Hamilton.
SPEEDWELL	30. 9.35	Hamilton Beardmore.

HMS Sharpshooter

HALCYON CLASS — NOTES

*FRANKLIN

3.4.45	Damaged in collision with US Tanker.
1946/52	Surveying in home waters.
1.53	Paid off to Reserve at Chatham.
56	BU by Clayton & Davie, Dunston-on-Tyne.

*GLEANER

14.3.45	In collision with a North Sea Pilot vessel.
3.45 to 4.45	Repaired at Chatham.
6.46	Reducing to Reserve at Devonport.
2.9.46	Paid off to Reserve at Falmouth.
20.4.50	Sold for scrap to Wards and BU at Preston.

HALCYON

10.45/1.46	Refit at Grimsby.
1.46/3.46	Repairs at Portsmouth.
5.46/6.46	Reserve at Devonport.
7.46/4.50	Reserve at Falmouth.
19.4.50	Sold for BU by Ward, Milford.

HARRIER

3.45	Refitting at Leith.
6.46/7.46	Armament removed at Chatham and reduced to Category C Reserve.
7.46/6.50	Reserve Fleet Harwich.
6.6.50	Sold for BU by King, Gateshead.

HAZARD

26.7.45	Damaged in collision with JASON in North Sea
9.45/10.45	Repairs to stern at Ipswich.
6.46/7.46	Armament removed at Chatham and reduced to Category 'C' Reserve.
22.4.49	Sold and BU by Ward, Grays.

JASON

3.45/4.45	Refitting on Thames.
26.7.45	Holed under the boat deck when in collision with HAZARD in North Sea.
9.45/10.45	Repairs at Portsmouth.
12.45/3.46	Repairs at Portsmouth.
8.46	Category 'C' Reserve at Portsmouth.
3.9.46	Sold to Wheelock Marden & Co. for conversion to cargo vessel. Renamed JASLOCK.
1950	BU at Grays.

SALAMANDER

27. 8.44	Attacked in error by typhoons off Cap d'Antifer; her stern was blown off and towed to the UK.
10.44	Reducing to Reserve at Hartlepool.
7. 5.47	Arrived Blyth for BU.

*SCOTT

3.46/6.46	Refitting at Sheerness.
6.46/11.46	Surveying in home waters.
22.4.47	In collision with Trawler PRINCE VICTOR—minor damage.
29.1.51	In collision with tug EXPELLER in the River Medway—damage to port side. Repaired at Chatham.
20.11.64	Arrived Chatham to pay off.
27.11.64	Arrived Portsmouth to lay up.
3.7.65	Arrived Troon to BU.

SEAGULL

9.45/11.45	Conversion to survey vessel at Rotterdam.
11.45/4.46	Completed conversion at Chatham.
6.46/1951	Survey home waters.
1.3.51	Reserve at Devonport.
1955	Hulk drill ship for Forth Division RNR Leith, Scotland.
1.5.56	Towed to Demelweek and Redding Plymouth for BU.

SHARPSHOOTER	5.46/3.46	Conversion to survey vessel on Thames.
	4.46	Repaired on Thames after collision with MV FEALTIE 3.4.46.
	1946/1947	Survey duties based at Singapore.
	13.10.47	In collision with MV CELEBES. Structural damage.
	1948-62	Based at Lowestoft surveying home waters.
	1.7.53	Renamed SHACKLETON, surveying west coast of England and Scottish waters.
	28.10.58	Aground in Bristol Channel, Asdic dome damaged.
	1961	Refit at Devonport, on completion survey duties. Bristol Channel and Irish Sea.
	9.11.62	Arrived Devonport for Reserve.
	3.11.65	Sold to West of Scotland Shipbreaking Co. Ltd. for BU.
	20.11.65	Arrived Troon.
SPEEDY	1.45/3.45	Refitting at Granton.
	3.6.46	Reducing to Reserve at Cairnryan.
	7.46	Category 'C' Reserve Milford Haven.
	5.11.46	Sold to HC Williams became Mercantile SPEEDON.
	1957	BU at Aden.
SPEEDWELL	2.3.45	In collision with CATHERINE, minor damage.
	10.45/12.45	Refitting at Grimsby.
	6.46/7.46	At Chatham disarming for Reserve.
	7.46	Category 'C' Reserve Harwich.
	5.12.46	Sold Societe Anonyme John Cockerill, became mercantile TOPAZ.
	11.5.54	Wrecked whilst en route Dutch Shipbreakers and BU at Dordrecht.

*   Completed as Survey Vessels but were converted back into minesweepers in 1939. At the end of the war "FRANKLIN" and "SCOTT" reverted to Survey vessels. "SHARPSHOOTER" and "SEAGULL" were similarly adapted.

HMS Worthing

BANGOR CLASS

Displacement:	656 tons.
Dimensions:	162 (pp) 174 (oa) x 28½ x 8¼
Machinery:	2 shaft geared turbines, SHP. 2,400 = 16 knots.
Armament:	1 - 3 in AA. 1 - 2 pdr. AA or 4 - 5″ AA (1 x 4) 2 - 20 mm AA guns.
Complement:	60.

Name	Completion Date	Builders
ARDROSAN	21. 5.42	Whites M.E. Blyth.
BANGOR	4.11.40	Harland & Wolff, Belfast.
BEAUMARIS	28. 8.41	Ailsa.
BLACKPOOL	7. 2.41	Harland & Wolff, Belfast.
BLYTH	17. 6.41	Whites, Blyth.
BOOTLE	23. 4.42	Ailsa.
BOSTON	26. 1.42	Ailsa.
BRIDLINGTON	5.10.40	Harland & Wolff, Belfast.
BRIDPORT	28.11.40	Harland & Wolff, Belfast.
BRIXHAM	19. 8.42	Whites M.E. Blyth.
BUDE	12. 2.41	Lobnitz.
DORNOCH	22. 7.42	Ailsa.
DUNBAR	3. 3.42	Whites M.E. Blyth.
EASTBOURNE	25. 5.41	Lobnitz.
FRASERBURGH	23. 9.41	Lobnitz.
HARWICH	20. 8.41	Parsons, Hamilton.
ILFRACOMBE	29. 3.42	Whites M.E. Blyth.
LLANDUDNO	5. 6.42	Whites M.E. Blyth.
LYME REGIS (ex Sunderland)	11. 9.41	Stephen.
PETERHEAD	9. 9.41	Whites M.E. Blyth.
POLRUAN	9. 5.41	Ailsa.
POOLE	8.10.41	Stephen.
RHYL	9.11.40	Lobnitz.
ROMNEY	3. 7.41	Lobnitz.
ROTHESAY	20.11.41	White, Hamilton.
RYE	19.12.41	Ailsa.
SEAHAM	4. 8.41	Lobnitz.
SIDMOUTH	17.11.41	Robb.
STORNOWAY	8.12.41	Robb.
TENBY	14.11.41	White, Hamilton.
WHITEHAVEN	20. 3.42	Philip.
WORTHING	22. 8.41	Philip.

BANGOR CLASS
NOTES

Name	Date	Notes
ARDROSSAN	29. 8.48	BU at Thornaby.
BANGOR	46	Transferred to Royal Norwegian Navy renamed "GLOMMA".
BEAUMARIS	1. 1.48	Sold and BU at Milford Haven.
BLACKPOOL	46	Transferred to Royal Norwegian Navy renamed "JANA".
BLYTH	49	Became Mercantile, renamed "RADBOURNE"
BOOTLE	6.49	BU at Charlestown.
BOSTON	6.49	BU at Charlestown.
BRIDLINGTON	46	Transferred to RAF (same name).
	6. 5.58	BU at Plymouth.
BRIDPORT	46	Transferred to RAF as "CAWLEY".
	6. 5.58	BU at Plymouth.
BRIXHAM	7. 7.48	BU at Dunston.
BUDE	46	Became Egyptian "NASR".
DORNOCH	1. 1.48	Sold and BU at Thornaby.
DUNBAR	1. 1.48	Sold and BU at Thornaby.
EASTBOURNE	10.48	BU at Dunston.
FRASERBURGH	3. 1.48	BU at Thornaby.
ILFRACOMBE	1. 1.48	BU at Dunston.
LLANDUDNO	47	Became Mercantile and named "RORVICK".
	52	BU.
LYME REGIS	24. 8.48	BU at Sunderland.
PETERHEAD	8. 6.44	Lost but later salved.
	5.48	BU at Peterhead.
POLRUAN	6.50	BU at Sunderland.
POOLE	1.48	BU at Pembroke Dock.
RHYL	10.48	BU at Gateshead.
ROMNEY	2.50	BU at Granton.
ROTHESAY	4.50	BU at Milford Haven.
RYE	9.48	BU at Purfleet.
SEAHAM	47	Became Mercantile (same name).
SIDMOUTH	18. 1.50	Sold and BU at Charlestown.
STORNOWAY	46	Egyptian "MATRUH".
TENBY	1.48	BU at Dunston.
WHITEHAVEN	1.48	BU at Briton Ferry.
WORTHING	7.48	BU at Dunston.

ALGERINE CLASS

Displacement:	850 tons.
Dimensions:	225' x 35½' x 9'.
Armament:	1 - 4", 4 - 40mm Bofors AA., (NIGER 1 - 4", 4 - 40mm Bofors AA., 2 - 20mm Bofors AA).
A/S Weapons:	4 DCT (1 Squid in HOUND, LENNOX, MUTINE and PLUTO instead of 4" guns) NIGER 2 DCT.
Range:	5,000 miles at 10 knots.
Complement:	85 (peacetime) 104 - 138 (war).

Name	PT No	Completed	Builders
ACUTE (ex ALERT)	M.106	30. 7.42	Harland & Wolff, Belfast.
ALARM	M.140	18. 5.42	Harland & Wolff, Belfast.
ALBACORE	M.101	16. 2.42	Harland & Wolff, Belfast.
ALGERINE	M.213	24. 3.42	Harland & Wolff, Belfast.
ANTARES (ex U.S.N.)	M.282	23. 8.43	Toronto.
ARCTURUS (ex U.S.N.)	M.283	23.10.43	Redfern.
ARIES (ex U.S.N.)	M.284	17. 7.43	Toronto.
BRAMBLE	M.273	28. 6.45	Lobnitz, Renfrew.
BRAVE	M.305	3. 8.43	Blyth.
CADMUS	M.230	16.10.42	Harland & Wolff, Belfast.
CHAMELEON	M.387	14. 9.44	Harland & Wolff, Belfast.
CHEERFUL	M.388	13.10.44	Harland & Wolff, Belfast.
CIRCE	M.214	16.10.42	Harland & Wolff, Belfast.
CLINTON (ex U.S.N.)	M.286	25. 8.43	Toronto.
COCKATRICE	M.229	10. 4.43	Fleming & Ferguson.
COQUETTE (ex BOWMANVILLE)	M.350	13. 7.33	Redfern.
COURIER (ex RCN ARNPRIOR)	M.349	31. 8.44	Redfern.
DISDAIN	M.442	21. 9.45	Lobnitz, Renfrew.
ESPIEGLE	M.216	1.12.42	Harland & Wolff, Belfast.
FANCY	M.308	21.11.43	Blyth
FANTOME	M.224	23. 1.43	Harland & Wolff, Belfast.
FELICITY (ex RCN COPPERCLIFFE)	M.369	10. 8.44	Redfern.
FIERCE	M.453	28.11.45	Lobnitz, Renfrew.
FLY	M.306	10.10.42	Lobnitz, Renfrew.
FLYING FISH (ex RCN TILLSONBURG)	M.370	14.10.44	Redfern.
FRIENDSHIP (ex U.S.N.)	M.398	15. 9.43	Toronto.
GOLDEN FLEECE (ex RCN HUMBERSTONE)	M.376	29. 8.44	Redfern.
GOZO (ex U.S.N.)	M.287	22.10.43	Redfern.
HARE	M.389	10.11.44	Harland & Wolff, Belfast.
HOUND	M.307	11.12.42	Lobnitz, Renfrew.
HYDRA	M.275	12. 2.43	Lobnitz, Renfrew.
JASEUR	M.428	27.10.44	Redfern.
JEWELL	M.390	9.12.44	Harland & Wolff, Belfast.
LAERTES	M.433	2. 3.45	Redfern.

Name	PT No	Completed	Builders
LARNE	M.274	22.11.43	Lobnitz, Renfrew.
LENNOX	M.276	18. 1.44	Lobnitz, Renfrew.
LIBERTY	M.391	18. 1.45	Harland & Wolff, Belfast.
LIGHTFOOT	M.288	19.10.43	Redfern.
(ex U.S.N.)			
LIONESS	M.377	11.12.44	Redfern.
(ex RCN PETROLIA)			
LOYALTY	M.217	22. 4.43	Harland & Wolff, Belfast.
(ex RATTLER)			
LYSANDER	M.379	21.11.44	Port Arthur.
(ex RCN HESPELER)			
MAENAD	M.435	11. 5.45	Redfern.
MAGICIENNE	M.436	11. 5.45	Redfern.
MAMELUKE	M.437	19. 3.45	Redfern.
MANDATE	M.438	22. 3.45	Redfern.
MARINER	M.380	23. 5.45	Port Arthur.
(ex RCN KINCARDINE)			
MARMION	M.381	29. 6.45	Port Arthur.
(ex RCN ORANGEVILLE)			
MARVEL	M.443	2. 4.45	Redfern.
MARY ROSE	M.360	24. 4.44	Redfern.
(ex RCN TORONTO)			
MELITA	M.289	20.12.43	Redfern.
MICHAEL	M.444	20. 5.45	Redfern.
MINSTREL	M.445	7. 6.45	Redfern.
MOON	M.329	6. 7.44	Redfern.
(ex RCN MIMICO)			
MUTINE	M.227	26. 2.43	Harland & Wolff, Belfast.
MYRMIDON	M.454	9. 7.45	Redfern.
MYSTIC	M.455	2. 8.45	Redfern.
NERISSA	M.456	28. 8.45	Redfern.
NIGER	M.442	21. 9.45	Lobnitz, Renfrew.
(ex DISDAIN)			
OCTAVIA	M.290	24. 2.44	Redfern.
ONYX	M.221	26. 3.43	Harland & Wolff, Belfast.
ORCADIA	M.462	11. 8.44	Port Arthur.
ORESTES	M.277	10. 4.43	Lobnitz, Renfrew.
OSSORY	M.463	3.10.45	Port Arthur.
PELORUS	M.291	7.10.43	Lobnitz, Renfrew.
PERSIAN	M.347	12.11.43	Redfern.
(ex U.S.N.)			
PICKLE	M.293	15.10.43	Harland & Wolff, Belfast.
PINCHER	M.294	12.11.43	Harland & Wolff, Belfast.
PLUCKY	M.295	10.12.43	Harland & Wolff, Belfast.
PLUTO	M.446	29. 9.45	Redfern.
POLARIS	M.447	29.10.45	Redfern.
POSTILLIAN	M.296	25.11.43	Redfern.
(ex U.S.N.)			
PROMPT	M.378	29. 9.44	Redfern.
(ex RCN HUNTSVILLE)			
PROVIDENCE	M.325	15. 5.44	Redfern.
(ex RCN FOREST HILL)			
PYRRHUS	M.448	31.10.45	Port Arthur.
RATTLER	M.217	22. 4.43	Harland & Wolff, Belfast.
RATTLESNAKE	M.297	23. 6.43	Lobnitz, Renfrew.
READY	M.223	21. 5.43	Harland & Wolff, Belfast.
RECRUIT	M.298	14. 1.44	Harland & Wolff, Belfast.

Name	PT No	Completed	Builders
REGULUS (ex RCN LONGBRANCH)	M.327	20. 5.44	Toronto.
RIFLEMAN	M.299	11. 2.44	Harland & Wolff, Belfast.
RINALDO	M.225	18. 6.43	Harland & Wolff, Belfast.
ROMOLA	M.449	3. 5.45	Redfern.
ROSAMUND	M.439	10. 7.45	Redfern.
ROSARIO	M.219	9. 7.43	Harland & Wolff, Belfast.
ROWENA	M.384	6. 9.44	Lobnitz, Renfrew.
SEABEAR (ex RCN St. THOMAS)	M.333	22. 6.44	Redfern.
SERENE (ex RCN LEASIDE)	M.354	14. 9.44	Redfern.
SKIPJACK (ex RCN SOLEBAY)	M.300	29. 4.44	Redfern.
SPANKER	M.226	20. 8.43	Harland & Wolff, Belfast.
STORMCLOUD	M.367	28. 3.44	Lobnitz, Renfrew.
SQUIRREL	M.301	16. 8.44	Harland & Wolff, Belfast.
SYLVIA	M.382	17. 5.44	Lobnitz, Renfrew.
TANGANYIKA	M.383	7. 7.44	Lobnitz, Renfrew.
THISBE	M.302	8. 6.44	Redfern.
TRUELOVE	M.303	3. 4.44	Redfern.
VESTAL	M.215	10. 9.43	Harland & Wolff, Belfast.
WATERWITCH	M.304	6. 8.43	Lobnitz, Renfrew.
WAVE	M.385	14.11.44	Lobnitz, Renfrew.
WELCOME	M.386	20. 1.45	Lobnitz, Renfrew.
WELFARE	M.356	4. 4.44	Redfern.

ALGERINE CLASS

Name	Dates	Notes
ACUTE	Jan 1945	Sweeping in Dardanelles with 5th MSF.
	Feb/May 1945	N.W. Italy, Leghorn; La Spezia & Genoa.
	Jun/Oct 1945	Refitting at Taranto.
	Jan 1946	Hit a wreck and lost a rudder, repaired at Genoa.
	9 May 1946	Left Malta for U.K.
	20 May 1946	Arrived Portsmouth.
	Sep/Oct 1946	Sweeping off Terschelling (Holland).
	Nov 1946	Reduced to Cat B reserve to lay up at Harwich.
	May 1956	Recommissioned into Dartmouth Squadron.
	July 1961	Paid off.
	1964	Towed to Malta and used as a torpedo target.
	Nov 1964	Broken up at La Spezia.

HMS Acute as Dartmouth Training ship—note classroom aft.

Name	Dates	Notes
ALBACORE	Jan 1945	12th MSF. Refit at Bizerta.
	Feb/Dec 1945	Clearance minesweeping from Naples, Leghorn and Genoa.
	Dec 1945/ Jan 1946	Refit at Gibraltar.
	Feb/Mar 1946	Minesweeping from Genoa.
	12 April 1946	Left Malta with other ships of the 12th MSF for U.K.
	May 1946	Refit at Chatham.
	Jun/July 1946	At Harwich for East Coast clearance sweeping.

Name	Dates	Notes

HMS Albacore — continued

	Aug 1946	At Portsmouth for sweeping in Channel.
	Sept 1946	At Terschelling (Holland) for sweeping.
	22 Oct 1946	With remainder of Flotilla withdrawn from active service. Refit at Portsmouth until Jan 1947.
	Jan 1947	Attached FOCBNG.
	April 1947	Cuxhaven for Operation 'Big Bang'.
	May/Sep 1947	Minesweeping from Cuxhaven.
	Oct 1947	Reduced to Cat B Reserve at Chatham.
	15 Aug 1963	Sold to Messrs Cordron of London for scrap.
	Sept 1963	Broken up at Port Glasgow.

HMS Albacore (as completed 1942)

ANTARES	Jan/Jun 1945	19th MSF, Sweeping channel to Trieste.
	July 1945	Damaged. "Near miss" from exploding mine.
	Jan 1946	Joined 5th MSF.
	May 1946	Returned to UK and USN Control (see CLINTON).
	29 Aug 1947	Sold to Potomac Shipwrecking Co, Potes Creek, Maryland.
ARCTURUS	Jan/Jun 1945	With 19th MSF in Adriatic.
	4 June 1945	Damaged internally, "near miss" by mine.
	11 June to 5th Sep 1945	Repairs at Taranto.
	Oct 1945	Malta.
	June 1946	At Devonport.
	10 Dec 1946	Control returned to USN, handed over to Executive Committee Surplus War Material.
	4 Mar 1947	Sold to Greece, renamed PYRPOLITIS (M76).

Name	Dates	Notes
ARIES	Jan/Jun 1945	With 19th MSF in Adriatic.
	2 July 1945	Mined whilst sweeping.
	July 1945/ Jan 1946	Repairs at Trieste
	Feb 1946	Rejoined 19th MSF.
	May 1946	To U.K.
	June 1946	Arrived Portsmouth and placed in reserve. Control returned to USN.
	4 May 1947	Sold by E.C.S.W.M. to Greece renamed ARMATOLOS (M12).

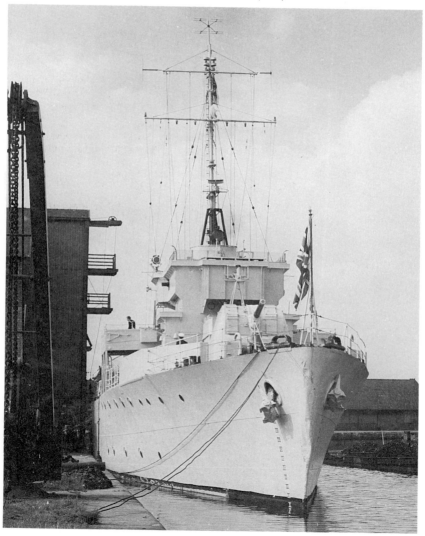

HMS Bramble (at Goole 1957)

Name	Dates	Notes
BRAMBLE	Oct 1945	Senior Officer 3rd MSF Rosyth/Londonderry.
	Jan 1946	Minesweeping in Irish Sea.
	Nov 1946	3rd MSF became 1st MSF at Plymouth.
	Mar 1951	S.O. 4th MSF assembled at Portland to work up, thence based at Harwich on depot ship MULL OF GALLOWAY.
	June 1953	Spithead Review.
	June 1955	Cuxhaven and Hamburg.
	Dec 1955/ Jan 1958	FPS.
	Aug 1961	BU at Gateshead.
BRAVE	Jan/Oct 1945	With 19th MSF in Adriatic.
	Nov 1945	Malta.
	26 May 1946	Sailed from Mediterranean for UK.
	June 1946	Reserve at Chatham then Harwich.
	1954	RNVR Tyne as SATELLITE.
	25 Nov 1958	BU at Dunston.
CADMUS	1.45-3.45	Minesweeping off Greece: Kinaros Channel and Doro Channel. (178 mines cut): Between Zea and Thermia Islands (131 mines).
	6.45-10.45	Sweeping in Gulf of Genoa.
	11.45-3.46	Malta/Gulf of Genoa/Malta.
	12.4.46	Left Malta with 12th MSF for Plymouth refit.
	6-9.46	At Harwich with 12th MSF sweeping off east coast, English Channel & Terschelling.
	10.46	Devonport for Reserve.
	1949	Towed to Chatham for refit to sale to Belgium.
	31.1.50	Officially transferred to Belgium and renamed GEORGES LECOINTE.

HMS Cadmus (1946)

HM Ships Chameleon, Plucky, Recruit & Rifleman (1954)

Name	Dates	Notes
CHAMELEON	Feb 1945	Far East to join 7th MSF.
	May 1945	Operation 'Dracula' (Rangoon).
	Jun/Aug 1945	Refit South Africa.
	Sept 1945	Singapore.
	August 1946	UK.
	13 Oct 1947	2nd MSF, Malta.
	Nov 1954	Sailed to UK with PLUCKY, RECRUIT and RIFLEMAN (see photo overleaf).
	13 Dec 1966	Arrived Portsmouth, placed in reserve.
	3 April 1966	Arrived Silloth for BU by Ardmore Steel of Cumberland.
CHEERFUL	Jan 1945	18th MSF sweeping off Dutch/Belgian coast.
	April 1945	Operation 'Dropkick' (Hamburg/Cuxhaven).
	May/Jun 1945	Ostend.
	August 1945	From Plymouth sweeping around UK.
	June 1947	With 3rd MSF (Firth of Forth).
	Oct 1947	Reserve at Devonport.
	July 1951	4th MSF.
	Oct 1952	Temp attached to F.P.S.
	15 June 1953	Spithead Review.
	Nov 1954	Reserve at Chatham.
	1963	BU at Queensborough.
CIRCE	June 1945 -Sept 1946	as for ALBACORE.
	Nov 1946	Reduced at Sheerness to lay up at Harwich.
	1948	Reserve at Harwich.
	Sept 1951	RNVR Drill Ship at Dundee.
	Dec 1966	BU W.H. Arnott, Young Co. Ltd., Dalmuir.
CLINTON	24 Sept 1945	Recommissioned after repairs following mining off Greece on 15 October 1944.
	Oct-Dec 1945	Sweeping (Salonika).
	1946	Mediterranean.
	7 Dec 1946	With ANTARES and FRIENDSHIP sailed for USA.
	Jan 1947	Returned to USN control.
	6 Nov 1947	Sold and scrapped.
COCKATRICE	Jan/Apr 1945	As CHEERFUL.
	May 1945	Operation 'Fireball' (Rotterdam).
	July/Aug	As CHEERFUL.
	Aug 1945	18th MSF Plymouth Command.
	Aug 1947	Transferred to 3rd MSF which became 1st MSF (Rosyth/Londonderry).
	Feb 1948	Reducing at Harwich.
	July 1951	4th MSF.
	May 1954	FPS.
	Nov 1954	Reserve at Chatham.
	1958/1959	Refitted as A/S Escort and fitted with Squid whilst in reserve.
	Aug 1963	BU at Inverkeithing.

HMS Coquette (January 1955)

Name	Dates	Notes
COQUETTE	Jan 1945	Mediterranean. Senior Officer 8th MSF after REGULUS sunk on 12 Jan 1945.
	April 1945	Leghorn/Genoa.
	August 1945	Malta.
	25 Aug 1945	To Far East.
	Oct 1945	Pacific Fleet, Hong Kong.
	March 1946	Mediterranean, Bizerta/Malta.
	Dec 1946	Reserve at Harwich
	April 1951	FPS.
	Nov 1956	Relieved by PALLISER.
	26 May 1958	BU at Rosyth.
COURIER	Jan 1945	Senior Officer 10th MSF.
	Feb 1945	Operation 'Shred' (Norway).
	Mar/Aug 1945	Operation 'Fireball' and sweeping off Holland.
	Sept 1945	Sailed for Far East Mineclearance based Singapore/Hong Kong.
	Jan 1946	Japan.
	Feb/Jun 1946	Sweeping off Borneo.
	28 July 1946	Sailed for the UK.
	Sept 1946	Arrived in UK and reserve at Harwich.
	25 Mar 1959	BU at Llanelly.
DISDAIN		Renamed NIGER in November 1944, (see NIGER).

Name	Dates	Notes
ESPIEGLE	1945/1946	As ALBACORE (12th MSF).
	March 1946	8th MSF, minesweeping Bizerta/Malta.
	Oct 1946 to 1948	Palestine Patrol.
	Dec 1946	5th MSF at Malta.
	1948	Reducing at Harwich.
	1952	Laid up at W. Hartlepool.
	1958/59	Refitted as A/S Escort whilst in reserve, fitted with Squid.
	1967	BU at Dalmuir.

HMS Espiegle

Name	Dates	Notes
FANCY	May 1945	Adriatic, 19th MSF.
	Dec 1945/ April 1946	Greece.
	June 1946	Arrived Chatham, transferred to FOCBNG at Cuxhaven.
	Dec 1946	Attached to HMS Vernon.
	Aug 1948	Paid off to Category B reserve at Devonport.
	3 April 1951 to 9 Aug 1951	Refitted at Woolston for Belgian Navy and renamed A.F. DUFOUR.
	1959	Hulked as a training ship (renamed NZADI) in Congo.
FANTOME	1945	At Devonport for repairs following mining off North Arica in 1943.
	1945/46	Reserve at Devonport.
	1947	Reserve at Milford Haven.
	22 July 1947	BU at Milford Haven.

Name	Dates	Notes
FELICITY	Jan 1945	10th MSF at Scapa Flow.
	April 1945	Loaned 18th MSF Hamburg/Cuxhaven for Operation 'Fireball'.
	July 1945	10th MSF Far East (Singapore/Hong Kong).
	July 1946	Refitting on the Tyne.
	Oct 1946	Sailed for Portland.
	1947	Mercantile as FAIRFREE.
	29 Aug 1957	BU at Charlestown.
FIERCE	4.46	Arrived Malta and allocated to 8th MSF.
	4.46-9.46	Minesweeping based at Bizerta. Used as VIP transport vessel to Naples etc.
	11.9.46	Joined (with 3 other Algerines and 4 destroyers) The Palestine Patrol.
	12.46	Left Malta for UK and refit at Portsmouth. On completion placed in Category 'A' reserve.
	9.47	Taken out of reserve & returned to Malta.
	1947-1953	Senior Officer. 2nd MSF.
	6.53	With others of 2nd MSF returned to UK to take part in Coronation Spithead review.
	7-8.53	Return to Mediterranean.
	11.53	Reserve Malta.
	2.8.59	BU at Gateshead.
FLY	1945	SO 12th MSF, Adriatic/Greece.
	May 1946	12th MSF Nore Command.
	Oct 1946	12th MSF disbanded, reduced to Category B Reserve at Devonport.
	Dec 1947	For disposal whilst in reserve.
	4 Oct 1948 to	Refitted at Chatham and renamed PALANG
	10 May 1949	on transfer to Iran.
	18 July 1949	Arrived Bahrein.
	Dec 1966	Taken out of service.
FLYING FISH	April 1945	11th MSF.
	Nov 1945	Sailed for East Indies where she served until Jan 1947 when the flotilla was renumbered as 6th MSF and paid off into Reserve at Singapore.
	August 1949	Commissioned as a tender to HMS TERROR for trials and Malayan patrol.
	Sept 1949	Transferred to Ceylonese RNVR.
	Nov 1949	Commissioned as VIJAYA.
	April 1975	Scrapped.
FRIENDSHIP	7 April 1945	SO 6th MSF sailed to East Indies with MELITA, POSTILLION, & PELORUS.
	April 1946	Returned to UK placed in Category B Reserve at Devonport.
	Jan 1947	Returned to USN and sold by them to Potomac Shipwrecking Co, Maryland.
GOLDEN FLEECE	Feb/Apr 1945	10th MSF.
	May 1945	11th MSF.
	March 1946	Sailed for East Indies.
	August 1946	Returned to UK and laid up in Reserve at Devonport.
	August 1960	BU at Llanelly.
GOZO	8 April 1945	Sailed to East Indies.
	May 1946	Category B Reserve at Chatham then handed over to USN Control and sold by the Executive Committee of Surplus War Material.
	4 May 1947	Sold to Greece, renamed POLEMISTIS (M74).

Name	Dates	Notes
HARE	Oct 1945	Sailed with 10th MSF to Far East.
	Sept 1946	Sailed from Far East to UK.
	Oct 1946	Arrived UK and placed in Reserve at Harwich.
	21 July 1959	To Royal Nigerian Navy, renamed NIGERIA, served at Flagship of Nigerian Navy.
	1962	Returned to RN.
	6 Nov 1962	Arrived Faslane to BU.
HOUND	Jan 1945	18th MSF, Plymouth Command.
	Jan 1947	3rd MSF, Rosyth.
	Sept 1947	Reserve at Devonport, refitted as A/S Escort whilst in reserve and fitted with Squid.
	Sept 1956	Commissioned to relieve RATTLESNAKE in FPS.
	March 1959	Relieved by MALCOLM.
	1 Sept 1962	BU at Troon.
HYDRA	10 Nov 1944	In the follow up to Operation 'Overlord' she was mined off Ostend and became a constructive total loss.
	1947	BU at Grays.
JASEUR	March 1945	1st MSF.
	17 May 1945	11th MSF.
	Nov 1945	Sailed for East Indies.
	Jan 1947	11th M/S renumbered 6th MSF, paid off into Category B Reserve at Singapore.
	April 1954	Sailed from Far East for UK, on arrival placed in Reserve at Chatham.
	26 Feb 1956	BU at Blyth.
JEWEL	1945	10th MSF Nore.
	Sept 1945 -July 1946	Far East.
	Sept 1946	Reserve at Portsmouth.
	Jan 1948	RNVR Drill Ship Tay Division.
	June 1955	Refitted at Devonport.
	28 Dec 1955	Commissioned for Dartmouth Squadron.
	Aug 1961	In reserve.
	7 April 1967	BU by T.W. Ward Ltd, at Inverkeithing.

HMS Jewel

Name	Dates	Notes
LAERTES	April 1945	11th MSF.
	Dec 1945	Sailed for East Indies and reallocated 10th MSF June 1946.
	Sept 1946	Returned to UK and laid up at Harwich.
	June 1953	Fleet Review at Spithead.
	21 April 1959	BU at Barrow.
LARNE	Aug 1945	Entered dock at Taranto with mine damage.
	Jan 1946	For disposal.
	7 Jan 1946	Transferred to Italy renamed ALABARDA.
	1951	Renamed AMMIRAGLIO MAGNACHI.
LENNOX	April 1945	6th MSF sailed for East Indies.
	May 1946	Returned to UK.
	Sept 1946 -Nov 1947	FPS.
	Feb 1948	Reserve at Portsmouth.
	Sept 1956	FPS.
	Feb 1958	Relieved by RUSSELL.
	1 June 1961	BU at Gateshead.
LIBERTY	May 1945/ Sept 1945	10th MSF Nore Command.
	Sept 1945/ July 1946	Far East Fleet.
	July 1946	Returned to UK.
	Feb 1948	In reserve at Devonport.
	1949	Taken out of reserve and refitted at Cowes.
	27 Nov 1949	Commissioned in Belgian Navy and renamed ADRIEN de GERLACHE.
	1970	BU Bruges.
LIGHTFOOT	8 April 1945	6th MSF sailed to East Indies.
	May 1946	Arrived UK and placed in Category B Reserve at Chatham, returned to USN Control whilst in reserve. Handed over to the Executive Committee of Surplus War Material.
	4 May 1947	Sold to Greece. Renamed NAVAMAHOS (M64).
	11 Dec 1973	Decommissioned, used as a target for guided missiles and sunk.
LIONESS	May 1945	SO 11th MSF.
	Oct 1945	Sailed for East Indies where she served until Jan 1947 when the flotilla was renumbered as 6th MSF and paid off into Reserve at Singapore.
	Feb 1954	Sailed for UK. On arrival placed into Reserve at Portsmouth.
	15 Nov 1956	BU at Rosyth.

Name	Dates	Notes
LYSANDER	1945	11th MSF.
	Jan 1946	Sailed for East Indies where whe served until Jan 1947 when the flotilla was renumbered as the 6th MSF and paid off in Reserve at Singapore.
	1950	Taken to Hong Kong for RNVR use and renamed CORNFLOWER.
	July 1951	Reverted to LYSANDER and rejoined 6th MSF.
	March 1954	Sailed for UK.
	June 1954	Refitted at Sheerness.
	18 April 1955	Commissioned for trials and Vernon Squadron as Minesweeping training ship.
	May 1956	Paid off into Reserve at Chatham.
	23 Nov 1957	BU at Blyth.

HMS Lioness

MAENAD	Jan/Apr 1945	Operation 'Shred'. Operation 'Crosskeys', Norway (40th MSF).
	May 1945	11th MSF.
	Nov 1945	Sailed for East Indies.
	Jan 1947	Paid off into Reserve at Singapore.
	June 1954	Sailed for UK and Reserve at Chatham.
	18 Dec 1957	BU at Grays.
MAGICIENNE	June 1945	From Canada for work up.
	Nov 1945	Sailed for East Indies with 11th MSF.
	Jan 1947	Reserve at Singapore.
	March 1954	Sailed for UK on arrival placed in Reserve at Devonport.
	20 Mar 1956	BU at Newport.
MAMELUKE	1945/1946	3rd MSF Rosyth and Londonderry.
	Jan 1947	1st MSF Reserve at Harwich.
	15 May 1950	BU at Middlesborough.

Name	Dates	Notes
MANDATE	Oct 1945	3rd MSF Rosyth and Londonderry.
	Jan 1947	1st MSF.
	5 Aug 1947	Reserve at Devonport.
	April 1951	4th MSF.
	May 1951	Portland for work up then based at Harwich.
	April 1952	Reserve at Devonport.
	Dec 1957	BU at Charlestown.
MARINER	July 1945	3rd MSF.
	Oct 1945	4th MSF.
	1946/56	FPS.
	18 April 1958	Handed over to Burma in London and renamed YAN MYO AUNG.
MARMION	Jan 1946	4th MSF, operating from Portsmouth, Norway and Londonderry.
	Oct 1946/ March 1947	FPS.
	1948	Reducing at Sheerness.
	August 1959	BU at Dunston.
MARVEL	Oct 1945	3rd MSF at Rosyth and Londonderry.
	Jan 1947	1st MSF.
	1948	Refit at Bristol, attached HMS Vernon.
	1953	From Reserve for Spithead Review.
	7 May 1958	BU at Charlestown.
MARY ROSE	Jan 1945	8th MSF Mediterranean (Greece).
	August 1945	With 8th MSF to Far East.
	March 1946	Mediterranean.
	Nov 1946	Returned to UK and Reserve at Chatham.
	14 Nov 1957	BU at Gateshead.
MELITA	7 April 1945	Sailed with 6th MSF for East Indies.
	July 1945	Operation 'Collie'.
	May 1946	Category B Reserve at Portsmouth.
	Feb 1948	Drill Ship for RNVR Tyne, renamed SATELLITE.
	1951	Renamed MELITA and refitted for reserve.
	25 Feb 1959	BU at Llanelly.
MICHAEL	Dec 1945	10th MSF East Indies Station.
	June 1946	11th MSF.
	Feb 1947	Paid off into Category B Reserve at Singapore.
	1950	Recommissioned for Malayan Patrol.
	May 1954	Sailed for UK and on arrival placed in Reserve at Portsmouth.
	15 Nov 1956	BU at Bo'ness.
MINSTREL	July 1945	10th MSF Nore Command.
	Nov 1945	10th MSF East Indies.
	Jan 1946	11th MSF.
	Feb 1946	7th MSF.
	June 1946	11th MSF.
	Feb 1947	Paid off into Category B Reserve at Singapore.
	April 1947	Taken out of Reserve and transferred to Thailand as PHOSAMTON on 20 Nov 1947.
	June 1953	Spithead Review.
	1982	Still in service.

Name	Dates	Notes
MOON	Jan 1945	8th MSF Mediterranean until October when the Flotilla joined the Pacific Fleet.
	March 1946	Mediterranean.
	Sept 1946	Palestine Patrol.
	May 1947	In Reserve at Harwich.
	13 Nov 1957	BU at Gateshead.
MUTINE	1945-1946	As ALBACORE (qv).
	10.46	Reducing at Sheerness for reserve at Harwich.
	4.56	Taken out of reserve to replace LYSANDER for service at Portsmouth in M/S training squadron. Later used as air target training ship.
	1958-59	Refitted as A/S escort vessel (4″ gun replaced by squid) whilst in reserve at Chatham.
	7.4.67	Towed to Barrow for breaking up.
MYRMIDON	Oct 1945	3rd MSF Rosyth and Londonderry.
	Jan 1947	3rd MSF renumbered as 1st MSF.
	Feb 1948	In Reserve at Devonport—thence Barry.
	2 Dec 1958	BU at Briton Ferry.

HMS Mutine (May 1958)

Name	Dates	Notes
MYSTIC	Jan 1946	3rd MSF.
	1947	Reserve at Portsmouth.
	3 May 1958	BU at Llanelly.
NERISSA	Jan 1946	3rd MSF Rosyth and Londonderry.
	Jan 1947	1st MSF.
	1948	Reserve at Harwich.
	Aug 1960	BU at Llanelly.
NIGER	March 1946	Sailed for East Indies, based at Penang and Singapore as HQ Ship.
	Dec 1946/ March 1947	Refitting at Devonport.
	April 1947/ Sept 1947	At Sheerness.
	Sept 1948	At Devonport reducing to Category A Reserve.
	1956	Transferred to Barrow in Furness Reserve.
	April 1960	Sold.
	Feb 1966	BU at Silloth.

HMS Niger (14.9.45)

OCTAVIA	1945	5th MSF in Mediterranean (Greece).
	1946/47	Palestine Patrol.
	July 1947	Arrived Devonport and reduced to Reserve.
	19 May 1950	BU at Gateshead.

Many long years were spent by ships of the class in Reserve. Here, *Myrmidon* **and** *Orcadia* **lie preserved at Barry (1956).**

Name	Dates	Notes
ONYX	1945	Hamburg/Cuxhaven.
	Sept 1945	Refit at Liverpool.
	Jan 1946	18th MSF Plymouth Command.
	March 1947	3rd MSF Port Edgar.
	August 1947	Reserve at Portsmouth.
	1956	Devonport Reserve.
	5 April 1967	BU at Inverkeithing.
ORCADIA	Jan 1946	4th MSF operating from Portsmouth, Norway and Londonderry.
	March 1947	Attached to Naval College Dartmouth for Cadet Training.
	1948	Reduced to Reserve at Devonport.
	1953	Spithead Review. Reserve at Barry.
	3 Dec 1958	BU at Briton Ferry.
ORESTES	1945	18th MSF Hamburg/Cuxhaven.
	Jan 1946	18th MSF Plymouth Command.
	Jan 1947	3rd MSF in Reserve Category B at Harwich.
	June 1956	FPS.
	April 1958	Relieved by PALLISER.
	April 1963	BU at Troon.
OSSORY	Jan 1946	4th MSF.
	1946-47	FPS
	1948	Reducing to Reserve at Portsmouth.
	4 March 1959	BU at Troon.
PELORUS	7 April 1945	Sailed for East Indies with 6th MSF.
	May 1945/ May 1946	Sweeping from Colombo.
	May/Aug 1947	Refitted at Chatham.
	Oct 1947	Sailed from Sheerness as PIETERMARITZ-BURG for South African Navy.
PERSIAN	8 April 1945	Sailed to East Indies with 6th MSF, operating from Trincomalee as escort vessel. Sweeping operations included Operation 'Collie' off Car Nicobar.
	May 1946	Catagory B Reserve at Portsmouth.
	Dec 1946	Returned to USN Control and sold for Mercantile use, renamed KIKIADES.
PICKLE	March 1945	Left UK as SO 7th MSF for East Indies.
	April 1945	Trincomalee.
	29 April 1945	Sailed with 7th MSF and 37th MSF as part of Assault Force in Operation 'Dracula' (Rangoon).
	Jun/July 1945	Refit South Africa.
	Sept 1946	Category B Reserve at Plymouth.
	April 1951	4th MSF Reserve at Harwich.
	30 July 1958	Sold to Ceylon, towed from Reserve at Portsmouth to be docked at Devonport.
	18 Aug 1958	Handed over at Devonport and renamed PARAKRAMA.
	1964	BU at Singapore.
PINCHER	Feb 1945	As PLUCKY (qv).
	Sept 1946	Category B Reserve at Harwich.
	May 1951	4th MSF at Portland for work up.
	Jan 1953	FPS.
	14 May 1953	Sailed from Chatham for Mediterranean.
	15 Sept 1953	Arrived Sheerness.
	March 1955	Completed refit at Chatham.

HMS Pickle

Name	Dates	Notes
	13 Sept 1955	Sailed for six week patrol off Iceland relieving WELCOME.
	12 Dec 1955	Reserve at Chatham.
	1960	At Portsmouth as fender hulk.
	7 March 1962	BU at Dunston.
PLUCKY	Feb 1945	Sailed from Falmouth with RIFLEMAN.
	April 1945	Trincomalee.
	29 April 1945	Sailed with 7th MSF and 37th MSF as part of Assault Force in Operation 'Dracula'.
	19 July 1945	Sailed to sweep the area around Phuket Island.
	24 July 1945	Exploded mine without warning (SQUIRREL sunk).
	26 July 1945	7th MSF attacked by Japanese A/C, VESTAL sunk.
	August 1945	as RIFLEMAN (qv).
	Sept 1946	Category B Reserve at Sheerness.
	1947	Malta 2nd MSF.
	April 1955	Placed in Reserve.
	15 Mar 1962	BU at Dunston.

Name	Dates	Notes
PLUTO	Jan 1946	4th MSF with MARMION (qv).
	Oct 1946/	
	March 1947	FPS.
	April 1947	Tender to HMS Vernon.
	1948	Minesweeping Trials Ship.
	1950s	Carried out trials with Squid A/S Mortar which was eventually fitted to other ships of this class.
	1953	Spithead Review.
	Dec 1954	In Reserve.
	1959-69	Accommodation ship at Barrow for crews of HMS HERMES & submarines under construction.
	1972	BU at Dalmuir.

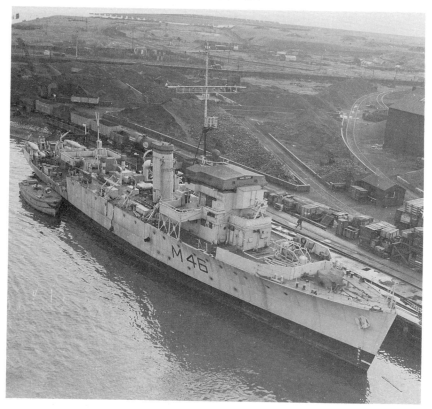

HMS Pluto in reserve having been fitted with Squid forward—in lieu of 4 inch gun.

Name	Dates	Notes
POLARIS	Jan 1946	3rd MSF Rosyth and Londonderry.
	Jan 1947	1st MSF.
	1948	Reserve at Devonport.
	26 Sept 1956	BU at Briton Ferry.
POSTILLION	7 April 1945	Sailed to East Indies with 6th MSF operating from Trincomalee.
	July 1945	Operation 'Collie'.
	May 1946	Returned to UK and whilst in reserve at Devonport, control returned to USN. Handed over to Executive Committee of Surplus War Material.
	4 May 1947	Sold to Greece renamed MACHITIS (M58).
	1980	Used as a target at Crete.
PROMPT	April 1945	MS HQ Ship for Operation 'Fireball'.
	9 May 1945	Mined off Ostend.
	1945	Paid off to Category C Reserve at Sheerness.
	16 Jan 1947	BU at Lower Rainham, Kent.
PROVIDENCE	Jan 1945	Mediterranean 8th MSF.
	August 1945	Far East.
	March 1946	Malta.
	Sept 1946	Palestine Patrol.
	1947	2nd MSF Malta.
	Feb 1948	Reducing at Harwich.
	17 May 1958	BU at Sunderland.
PYRRHUS	1946	4th MSF Londonderry.
	Dec 1947	Reserve at Devonport.
	1950	Attached to DEFIANCE.
	8 Sept 1956	Bu at Newport.
RATTLER		As LOYALTY (qv)
RATTLESNAKE	1945	As CHEERFUL (qv).
	Jan 1946	18th MSF Plymouth Command.
	Jan 1947	3rd MSF.
	Oct 1947	Reserve at Portsmouth.
	May 1951	4th MSF Portland to work up, thence to Harwich based on depot ship MULL OF GALLOWAY.
	Oct 1952-6	FPS, relieved by HOUND.
	Oct 1959	BU at Grangemouth.

HMS Rattlesnake

Name	Dates	Notes
READY	1945	SO 18th MSF. As CHEERFUL (qv).
	Jan 1946	Plymouth Command.
	Jan 1947	SO 3rd MSF Rosyth.
	1948	Reserve at Chatham.
	3 Mar 1951 -	Refitted at Cowes for Belgium and renamed JAN VAN HAVERBEKE.
	7 March 1961	BU at Bruges.

HMS Recruit

Name	Dates	Notes
RECRUIT	29 Apr 1945	Took part in Operation 'Broom' (the M/S section of Operation 'Dracula') with 7th MSF and 37th MSF.
	Jun/July 1945	Undergoing repair in South Africa with PICKLE and CHAMELEON.
	15 Aug 1945	With PLUCKY (SO), RIFLEMAN and PINCHER left Colombo to join Force 155 (6th MSF & 37th MSF) to sweep in the Malacca Straits.
	30 Aug 1945	Cleared the approaches to Sabang and Penang for battleship NELSON.
	Sep/Nov 1945	With 7th MSF Malaya and Penang area.
	Dec 1945	Sweeping Banka Strait.
	May/Jun 1946	South coast Malaya and Banguey Strait.
	July 1946	7th MSF transferred to BPF sweeping off North Borneo.
	Aug 1946	With PLUCKY, PICKLE, RIFELMAN, PINCHER & CHAMELEON left Colombo for UK.
	12.47-48	2nd MSF Mediterranean.
	1948-1953	Reserve.
	12.53	Taken out of reserve joined 2nd MSF as SO (Mediterranean).
	1954	To reserve.
	1962	At Barrow in reserve.
	1965	BU at Barrow.

Name	Dates	Notes
RIFLEMAN	Feb 1945	7th MSF sailed from Falmouth with PLUCKY for East Indies.
	April 1945	Trincomalee.
	29 April 1945	Sailed with 7th MSF & 37th MSF as part of Assault Force in Operation 'Dracula'.
	July 1945	As PLUCKY (qv).
	August 1945	Sweeping approaches to Singapore.
	June 1946	Singapore
	Sept 1946	Category B Reserve at Sheerness.
	1947	Refit at Portsmouth then allocated 2nd MSF.
	1948	Arrived Malta 2nd MSF.
	13 Dec 1954	Arrived Portsmouth with CHAMELEON, RECRUIT and PLUCKY, placed in reserve.
	1958/1959	Whilst in reserve refitted as A/S Escort.
	1971	Accommodation ship at Barrow.
	1972	BU at Barrow.

HMS Rifleman—at Malta.

Name	Dates	Notes
RINALDO	1945	SO 19th MSF Minesweeping Adriatic and Greece.
	June 1946	Returned to Portsmouth and placed in Reserve.
	May 1951	4th MSF Portland for work up thence to Harwich based on depot ship MULL OF GALLOWAY.
	1953	Spithead Review.
	12 Dec 1955	Reserve at Portsmouth.
	16 Aug 1961	BU at Gateshead.

HMS Rinaldo

Name	Dates	Notes
ROMOLA	1945	Allocated 3rd MSF.
	Oct 1945	Reallocated 4th MSF (see ORCADIA).
	Oct 1946/ May 1956	FPS
	June 1953	Fleet Review Spithead.
	June 1956	Relieved by ORESTES and placed in reserve at Devonport.
	19 Nov 1957	BU at Plymouth.
ROSAMUND	Jan 1946	4th MSF Londonderry/Portsmouth/Norway.
	1947	Reserve at Devonport.
	March 1947	Allocated for transfer to South Africa renamed BLOEMFONTEIN.
	5 June 1967	Sunk as a gunnery target by JOHANNESBURG and PRESIDENT KRUGER.
ROSARIO	1945	19th MSF as RINALDO (qv).
	May 1946	Transferred to FOCBNG Cuxhaven.
	Dec 1946	Training duties at Port Edgar.
	Dec 1947	Reserve at Port Edgar.
	3 June 1952/ 15 Jan 1953	Refitted at Hull for transfer to Belgium, renamed DE MOOR.
	May 1970	BU at Bruges.

Name	Dates	Notes
ROWENA	1945	As COQUETTE (qv).
	March 1946	5th MSF Malta.
	Sept 1946	Palestine Patrol.
	Feb 1948	2nd MSF Mediterranean.
	June 1951/58	Reserve at Malta.
	23 Oct 1958	BU at Gateshead.

HMS Rowena

Name	Dates	Notes
SEA BEAR	Mar 1945	5th MSF Mediterranean.
	August 1945	Far East.
	March 1946	5th MSF Malta.
	Nov 1946	Operation 'Retail' (Corfu).
	Dec 1946	Palestine Patrol.
	August 1947	Paid off at Chatham.
	12 Dec 1958	BU at Preston.
SERENE	Feb 1945	10th MSF Nore Command Operation 'Shred'.
	Oct 1945	Sailed for Far East.
	July 1946	Sailed from Far East to UK.
	Sept 1946	Arrived UK and Reserve at Devonport.
	8 Mar 1959	BU at Llanelly.
SKIPJACK	1945	As SEA BEAR (qv).
	Jan 1947	2nd MSF Operation 'Retail'.
	Sept 1947	Reduced to Reserve at Chatham for Harwich.
	1956	Reserve at West Hartlepool.
	March 1959	BU at Blyth.
SPANKER	1945	as RINALDO (qv).
	May 1946	Returned to UK from Mediterranean and transferred to FOCBNG at Cuxhaven.
	Dec 1946	Training duties at Port Edgar.
	Dec 1947	Reserve at Port Edgar.
	1952	Sold to Belgium.
	3 June 1952/ 25 Feb 1953	Refitted at Hull renamed DE BROUWER.
	1968	BU at Ghent.

HMS Serene at Hong Kong (Apr 46)

STORMCLOUD	1945	5th MSF Greece/Adriatic.
	1946/47	Palestine Patrol.
	Oct 1947	2nd MSF.
	Feb 1948	2nd MSF Mediterranean.
	Jan 1950	Reserve at Malta until 1958/59.
	2 Aug 1959	BU at Gateshead.
SQUIRREL	Jan 1945	Ostend as M/S HQ Ship.
	April 1945	7th MSF operating from Trincomalee.
	19 July 1945	Sailed for sweep round Phuket Island.
	24 July 1945	Sunk by gunfire after mining.
SYLVIA	1945	As STORMCLOUD (qv) 5th MSF.
	Nov 1946	Operation 'Retail' (Corfu).
	Aug 1947/ Jan 1950	2nd MSF Mediterranean.
	1950/1958	Reserve at Malta.
	24 Oct 1958	BU at Gateshead.
TANGANYIKA	1945	Sweeping off Holland/Belgium.
	March 1945	Operation 'Dropkick'.
	May 1945	Operation 'Fireball'.
	1948	Reserve at Chatham.
	15 Aug 1963	Sold to T.W. Ward for BU at Inverkeithing.
THISBE	1945	8th MSF Mediterranean.
	Aug 1945	Far East.
	March 1946	Arrived Malta.
	Feb 1948	Reserve at Harwich.
	Dec 1957	BU at Charlestown.

Name	Dates	Notes
TRUELOVE	1945	As SYLVIA (qv).
	Nov 1946	Operation 'Retail'.
	Jan 1947	2nd MSF.
	July 1947	Arrived Portsmouth for Reserve.
	Feb 1948	Reserve at Harwich.
	1949/1955	FPS.
	1955	Reserve at Chatham.
	23 Nov 1957	BU at Blyth.
WATERWITCH	1945/46	19th MSF. Adriatic/Greece.
	June 1946	To UK Reserve at Portsmouth.
	1958/59	Refitted as A/S Escort whilst in Reserve.
	9 Oct 1970	Sold to Gonzague Deckers, Antwerp.
WAVE	Jan 1945	10th MSF. Operation 'Shred'.
	Oct 1945	Sailed to Far East.
	July 1946	Returned to UK.
	Sept 1946	Arrived UK. Transferred to FPS Relieving EASTBOURNE.
	30th Sept 1952	Whilst sheltering in St. Ives Bay, Cornwall, anchor chain snapped during a gale, she was blown onto the sandy beach, then onto rocks and finally the sea front quay. Sixty-two of the 94 onboard were taken off by breaches bouy. The remaining 32 including the officers remained onboard. She was later towed to Devonport Dockyard, for repairs.
	Dec 1956/ July 1958	SO FPS.
	4th April 1962	BU Tyne.
WELCOME	May 1945	Joined 10th MSF.
	Oct 1945	Sailed to Far East.
	July 1946	Returned to UK.
	Sept 1946/ Dec 1957	FPS, relieving 'CARISBROOKE CASTLE'.
	Dec 1957	Reserve.
	3rd May 1962	BU at Gateshead.
WELFARE	Jan 1945	SO. 5th MSF for Operation 'Retail'
	1948	Reducing to Reserve at Portsmouth.
	June 1948	Commissioned to relieve 'FANCY' in Vernon Flotilla.
	June 1951	Tranferred to Lochinvar as M/S Experimental Ship.
	1953	Spithead Review.
	Dec 1955	Paid off to reserve.
	Nov 1957	BU at Grays.

HMS Wave at St Ives (September 1952).

BYMS

Displacement:	292 tons, 335 tons deep load
Dimensions:	130' (pp) 135½' (oa) x 24½' x 8½'
Machinery:	General Motors 2 — Shaft diesel. 1,200 bhp = 14 knots
Oil Fuel:	19 tons
Endurance:	2,500 miles at 10 knots
Armament:	1 - 3" AA. 2 - 20mm
Complement:	30

2,000 was added to pennant numbers between December, 1943 and April, 1944.

The story of the BYMS begins with lease-lend, this was the agreement Britain made with the U.S.A. before America entered World War Two. These ships were classed by the Americans as YMS, or Yard Minesweepers, prefixed with the letter 'B' for British, thus becoming BYMS.

One hundred and fifty ships were handed over to the Royal Navy. Numbers 1 to 80 were built for the R.N. and numbers 137 onwards were built for the U.S.N. However, numbers 137 to 284 were later transferred to the Royal Navy.

The BYMS were all built to the same basic design, numbers 1 to 134 had two thin funnels, 135 onwards had one large distinctive funnel.

All units were of an all wooden construction. Originally, they were fitted for both wire (Orophesa) and influnce sweeping.

BYMS 46

45

BYMS — FLOTILLA ALLOCATION

150th:	1945 - Copenhagen. 1946 - Dover.
151st:	1945 to 1946 Mediterranean.
152nd:	1945 - East Indies.
153rd:	1945-1946 Mediterranean.
154th:	1945 - West Africa.
155th:	1946 - Dover.
156th:	1945-1946 Mediterranean.
157th:	1945 - Yarmouth.
159th:	1944-1945. Normandy Invasion Force (ANCXF). 1946 - Dover.
160th:	1945-1946 Levant.
161st:	1945-1946 Eastern Fleet.
162nd:	1945-1946 Levant.
163rd:	1945 - North West Europe. 1946 - Lowestoft.
165th:	1945-1946 Harwich.
166th:	1945-1946 Eastern Fleet.
167th:	1945 - Humber & Dutch waters. 1946-1947 North West Europe.
168th:	1945 - East Indies.
169th:	1945-1946 Dover.
170th:	1945-1946 North West Europe.
180th:	1945-1946 South West Pacific.
181st:	1946-1947 East Indies & Singapore.
182nd:	1945 - Plymouth. 1945-1946 S.W. Pacific and Singapore.
183rd:	1946 Dover.

BYMS	Builders	Completion	Service Notes
1	America Car & Foundry, Wilmington	30. 5.42	1946 - Hartlepool. 10.12.46 - Returned U.S.N.
2	America Car & Foundry, Wilmington	22. 6.42	1946 - Pembroke. 8.47 - sold.
3	America Car & Foundry, Wilmington	13. 7.42	10.12.46 - Returned U.S.N.
4	America Car & Foundry, Wilmington	31. 7.42	1946 - Pembroke. 8.47 - sold
5	Wheeler Shipbuilders, Whitestone, New York	14. 9.42	1945 - 152nd. 1946 - Malaya. 12.11.46 - Returned U.S.N.
6	Wheeler Shipbuilders, Whitestone, New York	23. 9.42	1945 - 152nd. 1946 - Malaya. 12.11.46 - Returned U.S.N.
7	Wheeler Shipbuilders, Whitestone, New York	8.10.42	As BYMS 6 above.
8	Wheeler Shipbuilders, Whitestone, New York	19.10.42	As BYMS 6 above.

BYMS	Builders	Completion	Service Notes
9	Associated Ship Builders, Seattle	1. 9.42	1946 - 156th. 1946 - Malta. 5.47 - to Italy as 'ANEMONE'.
10	Associated Ship Builders, Seattle	31. 7.42	10.12.46 - Returned U.S.N.
11	Associated Ship Builders, Seattle	24. 9.42	1946 - Malta. 6.47 - sold.
12	Associated Ship Builders, Seattle	16.10.42	1946 - Malta. 23.5.47 - Returned U.S.N.
13	Associated Ship Builders, Seattle	30.10.42	1945 - 151st. 1946 - Malta. 5.47 to Egypt as 'GAZA'
14	Associated Ship Builders Seattle	24.11.42	As BYMS 13. 5.47 to Italy as 'GERANIO'.
15	Dachel Carter, Benton, Michigan	21. 7.42	1945 - 181st. 3.9.46. - Returned to U.S.N.
16	Dachel Carter, Benton, Michigan	9. 6.42	1946 - Pembroke. 1.48 - Sold.
17	Bellingham Marine	30. 5.42	1946 - Hong Kong. 1948 to China.
18	Bellingham Marine	16. 7.42	1946 - Hong Kong. 8.47 to U.S. Army.
20	Bellingham Marine	30.8.42	1946 - Malta. 6.47 - Sold.
21	San Diego Marine Construction	3. 8.42	1945 - 182nd. 1946 - 183rd. 1946 - Pembroke. 8.47 - Sold.
23	San Diego Marine Construction	31.10.42	1946 - Malta. 5.47 to Italy as 'MUGHETTO'.
24	San Diego Marine Construction	9.11.42	1945 - 151st. 1946 - Malta. 5.47 to Italy as 'NARCISO'
25	Ballard Marine, Seattle	14. 7.42	10.12.46 returned to U.S.N.
26	Ballard Marine, Seattle	20. 8.42	1946 - Malta. 6.47 - Sold.
27	Ballard Marine, Seattle	21. 9.42	1946 - 156th. 1946 - Malta. 5.47 - to Italy as'OLEANDRO'
28	Ballard Marine, Seattle	30.10.42	1945 - 151st. 1946 - Malta. 5.47 to Egypt as 'ARISH'
29	Barbour Boat Works, New Bern	8. 6.42	1945 - 150th. 1946 - Pembroke.

BYMS 29

BYMS	Builders	Completion	Service Notes
31	America Car & Foundry, Wilmington	13. 3.43	1946 - Malta. 6.47 - Sold.
32	America Car & Foundry, Wilmington	10. 4.43	1946 - Devonport. 1947 - Falmouth. 28.2.48 to Finland as 'TAMPAMMENPAA'
33	America Car & Foundry, Wilmington	4. 6.43	1.46 - to Greece as 'KALYMNOS'
34	America Car & Foundry, Wilmington	29. 6.43	1945 - 150th. 1947 - Pembroke. 8.47 - Sold.
35	America Car & Foundry Wilmington	14. 8.43	1946 - Sheerness 8.47 to Egypt as 'MALEK FUAD'
36	America Car & Foundry, Wilmington	20. 9.43	1945 - 182nd. 3.9.46 - returned to U.S.N.
37	Barbour Boat Works, New Bern	16. 3.43	1946 - Malta. 5.47 to Italy as 'ORCHIDEA'
38	Barbour Boat Works, New Bern	30. 4.43	1945 - 167th. 10.4.46 to Holland as 'MARSDIEP'.
39	Barbour Boat Works, New Bern	17. 6.43	1946 - Falmouth. 12.5.48 - returned to U.S.N.
40	Barbour Boat Works, New Bern	16. 8.43	1946 - Pembroke. 9.1.47 - returned to U.S.N.
41	Barbour Boat Works, New Bern	10.10.43	1946 - Sheerness. 8.47 to Egypt as 'DARFOUR'
42	Barbour Boat Works, New Bern	13.11.43	1945 - Portsmouth. 3.12.45 - returned to U.S.N.
43	Gibbs, Jackson, Florida	19.11.42	1945 - 182nd. 1945 - 181st. 3.9.46 - returned to U.S.N.
44	Gibbs, Jackson, Florida	29.12.42	1946 - 163rd. 1946 - Devonport 1947 - Falmouth. 28.2.48 to Finland as 'PURUNPAA'
45	Gibbs, Jackson, Florida	14. 1.43	1946 - Hong Kong. 31.7.46 - returned to U.S.N.
46	Gibbs, Jackson, Florida	3. 2.43	11.4.46 to Holland as 'WESTERSCHELDE'
47	Gibbs, Jackson, Florida	14. 2.43	1947 - Falmouth. 5.48 to Finland as 'KATANPAA'
48	Gibbs, Jackson, Florida	12. 3.43	1946 - 167th. 1.1.47 - returned to U.S.N.
49	Gibbs, Jackson, Florida	7. 4.43	1946 - Sheerness. 1947 -Falmouth. 5.48 - to Finland as 'VAHTERPAA'
50	Gibbs, Jackson, Florida	7. 4.43	10.4.46 to Holland as "HOLLANDSH DIEP"
51	Gibbs, Jackson, Florida	5. 5.43.	1946 - 165th: 1946—Pembroke 8.47 - sold.
52	Gibbs, Jackson, Florida	22. 5.43	1946 - Sheerness. 8.47 - sold
54	Gibbs, Jackson, Florida	29. 6.43	1.48 - sold.

BYMS 52

BYMS	Builders	Completion	Service Notes
55	Westergard, Tacoma	6. 5.43	1945 - 169th. 1946 -Sheerness. 1947 - Falmouth. 28.2.48 - sold.
56	Westergard, Tacoma	21. 6.43	1946 - 162nd. 27.4.46 to Greece as 'KARERIA'
57	Westergard, Tacoma	23. 7.43	1946 - Pembroke. 1.9.47 - returned to U.S.N.
58	Westergard, Tacoma	14. 8.43	1946 - Pembroke. 8.47 - to Greece as 'ARIADNI'
59	Westergard, Tacoma	30. 8.43	1945 - 181st. 1945 - 182nd. 1946 - Singapore. 24.8.46 -lost.
60	Westergard, Tacoma	14. 9.43	3.9.46 - returned to U.S.N.
61	Westergard, Tacoma	30. 9.43	1945 - 181st. 1945 - 182nd. 3.9.46 - returned to U.S.N.
62	Westergard, Tacoma	30.10.43	1945 - Devonport. 10.12.46 - returned to U.S.N.
63	Westergard, Tacoma	11.11.43	1945 - 181st. 1946 - 183rd. 1946 - Sheerness. 1947 -Falmouth. 2.48 - sold.
64	Westergard, Tacoma	22.11.43	1946 - Hong Kong. 31.7.46 - returned tp U.S.N.
65	Wheeler Shipbuilders, Whitestone, New York	22. 1.43	1945 to 1946 - 160th. 1969 - Deleted.
66	Wheeler Shipbuilders, Whitestone, New York	8. 2.43	1945 to 1946 - 160th 1946 - Greece.
67	Wheeler Shipbuilders, Whitestone, New York	23. 2.43	1946 - Greece
68	Wheeler Shipbuilders, Whitestone, New York	16. 3.43	5.46 - Greek 'LEFKAS' 1946 - 162nd. 1966 - Deleted.
69	Wheeler Shipbuilders, Whitestone, New York	30. 3.43	1945 - 169th. 1946 - Sheerness. 8.47 to Egypt as 'NAHARIA'
70	Wheeler Shipbuilders, Whitestone, New York	15. 4.43	1946 - Sheerness. 1947 - Falmouth. 6.5.48 - sold.
71	Wheeler Shipbuilders, Whitestone, New York.	4. 5.43	1946 - Pembroke. 8.47 - sold.
73	Wheeler Shipbuilders, Whitestone, New York	31. 5.43	1946 - 156th. 1946 - Malta. 5.47 - to Italy as 'BEGONIA'.
75	Wheeler Shipbuilders, Whitestone, New York	18. 6.43	1946 - 156th. 1946 - Malta. 5.47 - to Egypt as 'KAISARIA'.
76	Wheeler Shipbuilders, Whitestone, New York	26. 6.43	1945 - 165th. 1946 - Sheerness. 1946 - returned to U.S.N.
78	Wheeler Shipbuilders, Whitestone, New York	14. 7.43	1946 - Sheerness. 1.48 to Greece as 'VEGAS'
79	Wheeler Shipbuilders, Whitestone, New York.	25. 7.43	1946 - Falmouth. 5.48 - sold.

BYMS 68

BYMS	Builders	Completion	Service Notes
80	Wheeler Shipbuilders, Whitestone, New York	3. 8.43	1946 - Hong Kong. 31.7.46 - returned to U.S.N.
137	Astoria Marine, Construction	17. 4.43	1946 - Harwich. 11.46 - sold renamed 'CALISTO'
141	Astoria Marine, Construction	28. 8.43	1946 - Yarmouth. 1946 - 151st 1946 - Malta. 5.47 to Italy as 'DALIA'
142	Astoria Marine, Construction	30. 9.43	1946 - 163rd. 1946 - Sheerness. 11.47 to Italy as 'AZALEA'
148	Western Boat Builders, Tacoma	15. 5.43	1945 - 152nd. 1946 - M/S Force II Malaya, 11.10.48 -returned to U.S.N.
149	Western Boat Builders, Tacoma	5. 7.43	1945 - Wivenhoe. 1946 - 156th. 1946 - Malta. 5.47 - to Egypt as 'RAFAH'
150	Western Boat Builders, Tacoma	14. 8.43	1945 - Yarmouth. 1946 - 183rd. 1946 - Sheerness. 11.47 to Italy as 'GARDENIA'.
152	Campbell, San Diego	13.11.43	1946 - Pembroke. 1.48 - sold.
153	Campbell, San Diego	23.11.43	1946 - Hong Kong. 31.7.46.- returned to U.S.N.

BYMS	Builders	Completion	Service Notes
154	Campbell, San Diego	1. 1.44	1945 - Harwich. 25.8.45 - returned to U.S.N.
155	Berger, Manitowoc Wisconsin	4. 3.43	24. 5.46 - to Holland as 'VLIESTROOM'.
156	Berger, Manitowoc, Wisconsin	26. 3.43	10.4.46 - to Holland as 'TEXELSTROOM'
157	Berger, Manitowoc, Wisconsin.	29. 4.43	1946 - Pembroke. 4.48 - sold.
161	Berger, Manitowoc, Wisconsin	9. 8.43	1945 - 182nd. 1946 - M/S Force II Malaya. 11.46 -returned to U.S.N.
162	Berger, Manitowoc, Wisconsin	2. 9.43	1946 - M/S Force II Malaya. 12.11.46 - returned to U.S.N.
167	Dachel, Carter, Benton, Michigan	10. 8.43	1946 - Devonport. 1947 - Falmouth. 13.6.48. - sold.
168	Dachel, Carter, Benton, Michigan	7. 9.43	3.9.46 - returned to U.S.N.
171	H.C. Grebe, Chicago	8. 4.43	27.4.46 to Greece as 'KEFALINIA'
172	H.C. Grebe, Chicago	28. 4.43	15.4.46 - to Greece as 'KERKYRA'
173	H.C. Grebe, Chicago	15. 5.43	1946 - Devonport. 1947 - Falmouth. 13.6.48 - sold.
174	H.C. Grebe, Chicago	7. 6.43	1946 - Malta. 6.47 sold.
175	H.C. Grebe, Chicago	15. 6.43	1946 - Malta. 5.47 - Sold to Egypt - renamed 'TOR'
181	H.C. Grebe, Chicago	24. 9.43	1946 - Singapore. 3.9.46 -returned to U.S.N.
182	H.C. Grebe, Chicago	7.10.43	1945 - Buckie, 1946 - 183rd. 1946 - Sheerness. 1.48 - sold.
185	H.C. Grebe, Chicago	9. 2.43	1946 - Greek Navy.

BYMS 172

BYMS	Builders	Completion	Service Notes
186	Greenpoint Basin, Long Island	20. 2.43	1946 - Greek Navy.
187	Greenpoint Basin, Long Island	12. 3.43	1946 - Malta. 6.47 - Sold, renamed 'LORD STRICKLAND'.
188	Greenpoint Basin, Long Island	30. 3.43	1946 - 167th. 2.47 - to Holland as 'VOLKERAK'.

BYMS 188

189	Greenpoint Island, Long Island	1. 5. 43	1946 - 163rd. 1946 - Devonport. 8.47 - sold.
190	Greenpoint Basin, Long Island	10. 5.43	3.46 - sold.
194	Greenpoint Basin, Long Island	12. 7.43	1946 - Sheerness. 1.47 - to Italy as 'TULIPANO'.
202	C. Hiltebrant, New York	11. 8.43	1946 - Sheerness.1.48 - sold.
203	C. Hiltebrant, New York	31. 9.43	1946 - M/S Force II Malaya, 12.11.46 - returned to U.S.N.
204	C. Hiltebrant, New York	14. 9.43	3.9.46 - returned to U.S.N.
205	C. Hiltebrant, New York	29. 9.43	1946 - Singapore. 3.9.46 -returned to U.S.N.
206	C. Hiltebrant, New York	16.10.43	1946 - 182nd. 1946 - Malta. 5.47 - to Italy as 'MAGNOLIA'
209	Robert Jacob, City Island, New York	24. 3.43	15.4.46 - to Greece as 'ZAKYNTHOS'
210	Robert Jacob, City Island, New York	19. 4.43	10.4.46 - to Holland as 'BORNDIEP'
211	Robert Jacob, City Island, New York	7. 5.43	1946 - Sheerness. 8.47 - sold to Poland.

BYMS	Builders	Completion	Service Notes
212	Robert Jacob, City Island, New York	29. 5.43	1946 - 156th. 1946 - Malta. 5.47 to Egypt as 'KORDOFAN'
213	Robert Jacob, City Island, New York	18. 6.43	1945 - 169th. 1946 - Pembroke. 14.5.48 - returned to U.S.N.
214	Robert Jacob, City Island, New York	2. 7.43	1945 - 150th. 1946 - Sheerness. 10.12.46 Returned USN
217	J.M. Martinac, Tacoma	29. 4.43	1945 - 152nd. 28.5.46 - returned to U.S.N.
221	J.M. Martinac, Tacoma	16. 9.43	1945 - 150th. 1946 - Sheerness. 22.10.47 - sold.
223	Mojean & Erikson, Tacoma	28. 6.43	1945 - 152nd. 1946 - M/S Force II Malaya. 12.11.46 -returned to U.S.N.
225	Mojean & Erikson, Tacoma	14.10.43	1946 - 182nd. 1946 - M/S Force II Malaya. 12.11.46 returned to U.S.N.
229	Sample, Booth Bay, Maine	6. 5.43	12.43 - Greek 'PATMOS'
230	Sample, Booth Bay, Maine	7. 7.43	1945 - 167th. 1.1.47 - returned to U.S.N.
232	Sample, Booth Bay, Maine	8. 9.43	11.10.46 - returned to U.S.N.
233	Sample, Booth Bay, Maine	8.10.43	1946 - Sheerness. 1.48 - sold.
234	Sample, Booth Bay, Maine	3.11.43	1945 - 182nd. 1946 - 183rd. 1946 - Pembroke. 14.5.48 -returned to U.S.N.
236	Stadium Yacht Co., Cleveland	26. 6.43	1946 - Singapore. 9.3.46 - returned to U.S.N.
240	Stadium Yacht Co., Cleveland	25. 5.43	7. 5.46 - Greek 'ITHAKI'
244	Tacoma Boat Building Co.	3. 7.43	1945 - 181st. 1946 - Singapore. 1946 - M/S Force II Malaya. 14.11.47 - sold.
246	Tacoma Boat Building Co.	27. 8.43	1946 - Hong Kong. Cannibalised.
252	Weaver Shipyard, Orange, Texas	29. 9.43	1946 - Pembroke. 10.6.47 - returned to U.S.N.
253	Weaver Shipyard, Orange, Texas	22.10.43	1945 - 159th. 1946 - Sheerness. 1947 - Falmouth. 5.6.48 - Sold.
254	Weaver Shipyard, Orange, Texas	12.11.43	1945 - 167th. 1.1.47 - returned to U.S.N.
256	Weaver Shipyard, Orange, Texas	20.12.43	1945 - Inverness. 1946 - 183rd. 1946 - Sheerness. 1.48 - sold.
257	Weaver Shipyard, Orange, Texas	20. 1.44	1945 - Harwich. 1946 - 183rd. 1946 - Sheerness. 8.47 - sold Poland.
258	Weaver Shipyard, Orange, Texas	8. 2.44	1945 - Lowestoft. 1945 - 182nd. 1946 - M/S Force II Malaya. 12.11.46 - returned to U.S.N.
261	South Coast C, Newport, California	9. 7.43	1945 - 165th. 1946 - Pembroke. 8.47 - sold.
264	South Coast C, Newport, California	26.10.43	1945 - 182nd. 1946 - M/S Force II Malaya. 10.11.46 - returned to U.S.N.

BYMS	Builders	Completion	Service Notes
277	J.M. Martinac, Tacoma	18.10.43	1946 - Sheerness. 11.47 - to Italy as 'FIORDALISO'
278	J.M. Martinac, Tacoma	13.11.43	1946 - Sheerness. 1.47 to Italy as 'PRIMULA'
279	H.C. Grebe, Chicago	16.10.43	1945 - Peterhead. 1946 -150th. 1946 - Sheerness. 1947 - Falmouth. 6.5.48 -sold.
280	H.C. Grebe, Chicago	30.10.43	1945 - Peterhead. 1946 -Sheerness. 11.47 - to Italy as 'VERBENA'.
282	San Diego Marine Construction	26. 8.43	1946 - 163rd. 1946 -Devonport. 8.47 to Poland.
284	San Diego Marine Construction	2.11.43	1945 - 182nd. 1946 - 180th. 1946 - Hong Kong. 31.7.46 -returned to U.S.N.

MOTOR MINESWEEPERS
105' CLASS

Admiralty Type:	No's 1-118, 123-313 (1,500 added to original numbers).
Displacement:	165 tons.
Dimensions:	105 (pp) 119 (oa) x 23 x 9½ '
Speed:	11 knots.
Armament:	2 - 5" (1 x 2) M.G.'s.
Complement:	20.

Built between 1940-1944 of wooden construction it was a safer vessel than the steel trawlers for sweeping magnetic mines, but their towing capacity was poor. They were adequate for the LL sweep but not so good for wire sweeping. Later the SA (an acoustic sweep) hammer box was added, this was mounted on the boom which was lowered over the bow.

Requisitioned craft	
No's:	119-122.
Displacement:	216 tons gross.
Dimensions:	116 (pp) 130 (oa) x 26 x 10'.
Speed:	8 knots.
Armament:	2-.303" (2 x 1) M.G.'s.

These four were built during 1941-42 and were renamed 'EMBERLEY', 'ODERIN', 'MARTICOT', 'MERASHEEN' as danlayers.

105 Class
(1500 added to original numbers in 1947)

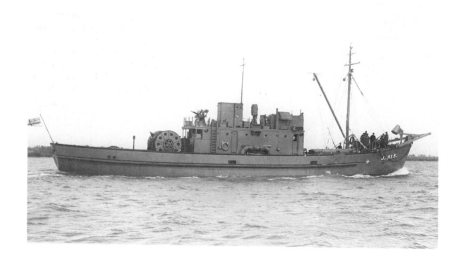

MMS	Builders	Completion Date	Notes
1.	Richards Iron Works, Lowestoft.	19.11.40	1946 Greece renamed CHIMARRA.
2.	G. Forbes, Peterhead.	19. 4.41	1945 — 116th M/S. 1946 — Sold.
5.	Camper & Nicholson, Gosport.	11. 5.41	1946 to 1951 transferred to Greece (MIKONOS), 1.10.56 — Sold.
6.	J.W. & A. Upham, Brixham.	1. 6.41	1946 sold renamed OYLAND.
9.	P.K. Harris, Appledore.	24. 3.41	1945-47 Transferred to France (D.364). 6.4.48 sold.
10.	Wilson Noble, Fraserburgh.	30. 5.41	1946/50 to Italy. 9.50—TRV 20 Malta. 26.5.56 Sold.
14.	W. Reekie, St. Monance.	5.41	1946 sold.
15.	Wivenhoe Shipyard.	22. 3.41	1946 sold.
16.	Wivenhoe Shipyard.	30. 4.41	1946 sold renamed TASS.
17.	Wivenhoe Shipyard.	30. 5.41	1946 sold.
18.	Philip & Sons, Dartmouth.	12.40	1946 sold renamed FJELLHEIM.
19.	Richards Iron Works, Lowestoft.	2.41	1945 to Humber Sea Cadets.
20.	G. Forbes, Peterhead.	3. 6.41	1946 At Malta. 7.46 sold.
21.	Herd & Mackenzie, Buckie.	11. 6.41	1945-47 France as D.241. 12.47 at Chatham. 1948 sold.
22.	Husband Yacht Yard, Marchwood.	22.11.41	3.46 for sale.
26.	F. Curtis, Par.	4. 8.41	1946 renamed SKAVSEN.
28.	F. Curtis, Par.	14. 9.41	1945 at Sheerness. 1946 sold renamed HORDABO.
29.	Camper & Nicholson, Gosport.	7.41	1946 for sale.
31.	W. Reekie, Anstruther.	6.41	1946 for sale.
32.	Macduff Eng. & Ship Bldrs. Co.	8.41	2/46-3/50 Italy as DR202., 1950 at Malta, 1951—108th M/S. 3.6.55 sold.
33.	J & G Forbes, Sandhaven.	20. 6.41	1946 at Malta, 7/46 sold.
34.	J. Noble, Fraserburgh.	10. 7.41	1945 at Malta, 1946-49 Italy as DR203., 1951—108th M/S. 1952 at Malta, 10.55 sold.

MMS 1534 at Malta (July 1951)

MMS	Builders	Completion Date	Notes
35.	Wilson Noble, Fraserburgh.	10. 8.41	1945 at Malta, 1946-49 Italy as DR204., 1954 Chatham. 22.2.55 sold.
36.	Wivenhoe, Shipyard.	12. 4.41	1946-48 Danish Navy. 1948 Chatham. 1951-120th M/S. 1952 China. 11.58 sold BU.
37.	Wivenhoe, Shipyard.	18. 8.41	11.45—143rd M/S. 12.45 Falmouth. 2.46 Salcombe. 1946 sold renamed STENSUND.
38.	P.K. Harris, Appledore.	6. 8.41	1946 Malta. 7.46 sold.
40.	Richards Ironworks, Lowestoft.	10. 6.41	1951 Renamed RITA.
41.	Richards Ironworks, Lowestoft.	28. 7.41	1946 Sheerness, 1946 sold renamed VAEREN.
42.	F. Curtis, Looe.	18. 7.41	1945—138th M/S. 1946 sold renamed ALVALD.
43.	F. Curtis, Looe.	5. 9.41	2.44-5.46—118th M/S (Belgium). 7.46 Sheerness. Sold.
44.	Richards Ironworks, Lowestoft	18. 9.41	1946 sold renamed FLATHOLM
45.	Richards Ironworks, Lowestoft	10.41	1946 sold renamed EIHOLM. 16.12.48—lost
46.	J.L. Bolson, Poole.	25.11.41	1946-51 Greek Navy as TEPELINI. 1952 Chatham, 1957 sold.
47.	J.W. & A. Upham, Brixham.	18. 8.41	1945 French Navy as D363. 1947 Chatham, 1950 for sale.
48.	J.W. & A. Upham, Brixham.	13.10.41	1946-50 Italian Navy as DR205, 1950 Malta. 10.55 sold.
49.	J. Morris	7. 4.42	1945—119th M/S. 1945-47 French Navy as D377, 11.47 Portsmouth. 1950 sold.
50.	Clapson & Sons, Barton-on-Humber	23. 8.41	1946-49 Italian Navy as DR206, 1949 Malta. 1954 Chatham. 10.54 sold for BU.
53.	Herd & Mackenzie, Buckie.	10.10.41	1945 DGV at Malta. 1946-51 Greek Navy as KORYTSA. 1951 Malta. 1952 Chatham. 1954 Gibraltar. 1.10.56 sold.
54.	Herd & Mackenzie, Buckie.	25.12.41	1945—139th M/S. 1946 sold to Dutch Navy.
56.	J. Noble, Fraserburgh.	21.10.41	1946 Chatham. 1951—120th M/S Nore. 1952—120th M/S Hong Kong. 1954 Hong Kong RNVR. 5.59 sold.
57.	J. Noble, Fraserburgh.	22. 2.42	1946 Chatham. 1951—104th M/S. 1953 Portsmouth. 1954 Gibraltar. 3.1.57 sold.

MMS	Builder	Completion Date	Notes
58.	J.L. Bolson, Poole.	30. 4.42	1946-51 Greek Navy as ARGYROKASTION. 1952 Chatham. 2.54 Thames RNVR. 17.4.54 Lost by fire off Dunkirk.
59.	J & G Forbes, Sandhaven.	12. 9.41	1946 sold.
60.	J & G Forbes, Sandhaven.	27.11.41	1946 sold.
61.	Macduff Eng. & Ship Bldrs Co.	14.12.41	3.46 for sale.
62.	Macduff Eng. & Ship Bldrs Co.	15. 6.42	1945—144th M/S. 11.45 sold renamed STYRFJELL.
63.	W. Reekie, St. Monance.	2.42	22.2.46 To Turkey renamed BAFRA.
65.	Husband Yacht Yard, Cracknor.	27. 7.42	14.5.46 to Turkey renamed BANDIMA.
67.	Husband Yacht Yard, Cracknor	29.11.42	1945-47 French Navy as D375. 30.1.48 sold.
69.	Richards Ironworks, Lowestoft	19. 2.42	1946—101st M/S, 1947 Chatham. 1951—104th M/S. 4.54 sold as houseboat.
71.	East Anglian Constr., Oulton Brd.	6.42	1946 sold renamed HEPO.
72.	East Anglian Constr., Oulton Brd.	5.42	1946 sold renamed VARTDAL.
74.	F. Curtis, Par.	19.10.41	1946 sold renamed KLUNGSHOLM.
75.	F. Curtis, Par.	16.11.41	1945—118th/MS. 1946 Sheerness. Sold renamed EVERI.
79.	G. Forbes, Peterhead.	21. 9.41	1945—113th M/S. 1945—118th M/S. 1946—102nd M/S. 1947—Chatham. 1951—120th M/S. 1952—108th M/S Malta. 1952 China 120th M/S. 1954 Hong Kong RNVR. 5.59 sold in China.
80.	G. Forbes, Peterhead.	21.11.41	14.2.46 sold.
81.	G. Forbes, Peterhead.	21. 2.42	1.46 for sale.
83.	Wivenhoe Shipyard Ltd.	22.12.41	1946-1949 Danish Navy. 15.1.57 sold for BU.
84.	Wivenhoe Shipyard Ltd.	23. 2.42	1945—132nd M/S. 1945-48 Danish Navy, 1949 Chatham, 1951—120th M/S China, 1954 Hong Kong, 1958 BU Hong Kong.
85.	Wivenhoe Shipyard Ltd.	10. 7.42	7.46 Sold.
86.	Wivenhoe Shipyard Ltd.	10. 9.42	1945-46 Danish Navy, 1947 Chatham, 1952 Portsmouth, 1953 Chatham, 19.6.59 Air Ministry.
87.	Wivenhoe Shipyard Ltd.	27.10.42	1945—117th M/S. 1946—102nd M/S. 9.12.56 Sold (Mercantile).
88.	Philip & Sons, Dartmouth.	16. 3.42	22.4.46 to Turkey renamed BARTIN.
91.	J. Morris	27.11.42	1945/47 to France. 1948 sold.

MMS	Builders	Completion Date	Notes
97.	Brunton, Cochin.	9. 3.42	29.11.46 sold.
98.	Brunton, Cochin.	22. 3.42	29.11.46 sold.
99.	Wagstaff & Hatfield, Canada.	24.11.42	1946/50 to Italy, 1950 Malta, 1952 Gibraltar, 1953 Chatham, 3/55 sold (houseboat) Medway.
100.	Wagstaff & Hatfield, Canada.	16.12.42	1949/50 to Italy, 1950 Malta, 1952 Gibraltar, 1953 Portsmouth. 8.55- sold.
102.	Wagstaff & Hatfield, Canada.	28. 8.42	1945/50 to Italy, 1950 Malta, 1952 Gibraltar, 1953 Portsmouth, 1954 Pembroke Dock. 1956 sold.
103.	Shelburne Company, Nova Scotia	30. 9.42	(As MMS 101 to 1952). 1953 Chatham. 10.56 sold.
104.	Clare Shipbuilding Co., Metaghan	4. 7.42	1946/51 to Italy, 1951 Malta, 1952 Gibraltar, 25/2/54 sold.
105.	Clare Shipbuilding Co., Metaghan	4. 7.42	1946/51 to Italy, 1951 Malta, 1952 Gibraltar, 25/2/54 sold.
106.	Clare Shipbuilding Co., Metaghan	4. 7.42	As MMS 104 to 1952, 1953 Chatham, 12/1/56 sold.
107.	Chantiers Marit., St. Laurent.	25. 8.42	2/47 Singapore, 4/47 Presumed lost.
108.	Chantiers Marit., St. Laurent.	26. 8.42	As MMS 107.
109.	J. Morris.	12.10.42	1946—101st M/S, 1947 Chatham, 1950—301st M/S., 1951—51st M/S, 1954 Rosyth, 8/56 sold.
110.	J. Morris.	23.11.42	1945—117th M/S., 1947 Chatham, 1951—104th M/S., 1953 Chatham, 10/1/56 sold.
112.	J. Morris.	15. 3.43	3/1/47 sold.
114.	Wivenhoe Shipyard	23.4.42	1946 sold.
116.	J.S. Doig, Grimsby.	13.12.42	1945/47 French Navy as D365. 1948 sold.
118.	J.S. Doig, Grimsby	14.6.42	1945/47 French Navy as D366. 12/47 Chatham for sale.
121.	H. Stone, St. Johns, Newfoundland.	12. 9.41	1948 for sale.
122.	H. Stone, St. Johns, Newfoundland.	12. 9.41	1/46 for sale.
129.	Brunton, Cochin.	5.43	1948 Royal Indian Navy as MUJAHID. 1950 sold.
130.	Brunton, Cochin.	43	Royal Indian Navy. 1954 sold.
131.	Brunton, Cochin.	3.44	8/48 Royal Indian Navy as GHAZI.
132.	Brunton, Cochin.	1.44	10/44 Royal Indian Navy as BARQ.
133.	Wilson Noble, Fraserburgh.	29. 1.42	1945/47 French Navy as D367. 12/47 for sale.
134.	Wilson Noble, Fraserburgh.	13. 4.42	1945/46 French Navy as D368.

MMS	Builders	Completion Date	Notes
135.	Clapson & Sons, Barton on Humber.	31. 3.42	1946/49 Italian Navy as DR212, 1951—108th M/S, 1953 Malta. 11.55 sold renamed QUEEN OF PEACE.
137.	Husband Yacht Yard, Marchwood.	8. 3.43	5/46 for sale, sold renamed BRATTAS.
138.	Husband Yacht Yard, Marchwood.	10. 5.43	1943/46—139th M/S. Disposal unknown.
140.	F. Curtis, Par.	1. 3.42	4.46—to Turkey.
141.	Steers, St. John, Newfoundland.	12. 1.43	1946 Lowestoft. 1947 sold.
142.	Steers, St. John, Newfoundland.	12. 1.43	1946 Lowestoft. 11/46 for sale.
143.	Colombo Port Commissioners.	27. 6.45	1945—143rd M/S., 1945—146th M/S., 1946/47 Greek Navy as THIOS, 1947 sold at Malta.
144.	Colombo Port Commissioners.	11.10.44	1946/51 Greek Navy as TINOS, 1953 Chatham, 30/1/57 sold BU.
145.	Cargo Boat Despatch Co., Colombo.	45	4/45 Royal Indian Navy, 1946 sold.
148.	Bombay/Burma Trading Co. Rangoon.	46	29.11.46 sold in India.
149.	F. Curtis, Par.	22. 3.42	1946—101st M/S, 8/46 for sale, sold renamed SOLBRIS.
150.	F. Curtis, Par.	3. 5.42	7/46 to Turkey.
151.	Irrawadi Flot Co, Rangoon	19.12.45	1945 Royal Indian Navy, 11.49 for sale.
154	Rangoon Dockyard	28. 1.46	1945 Royal Indian Navy, 1949 Bombay Reserve.
167	F. Curtis, Par.	17. 5.42	1946-1950 Italian Navy as DR213, 1946/50 Malta, 2.12.55 Sold.
169	F. Curtis, Par.	8. 8.42	1946 Sold.
172	F. Curtis, Totnes	10. 6.42	1946-1950 Italian Navy as DR214. 1950 Malta, 1951 108th M/S. 1955 sold— renamed 'PINU'.
174	J.W. & A. Upham, Brixham	6. 7.42	1946—104th M/S, 1951 to Jugoslavia.
177	Richards Iron Works, Lowestoft	17.11.42	1945 Dover, 1946 sold, renamed 'PERODD'.
178	Richards Iron Works, Lowestoft	28. 1.42	1946 sold.
179	J.S. Doig, Grimsby	27. 7.42	1946 sold.
181	Clapson & Sons, Barton-on-Humber	20. 7.42	1946—104th MSS, Feb 1958 sold.
182	W. Reekie, St Monance	11.10.42	1946—118th MSS, 1950 Belgium.
183	P.K. Harris, Appledore	20.10.42	March 1946 for sale.
184	G. Forbes, Peterhead	23. 5.42	Oct 1947—France as D362. 1948 sold.

MMS	Builders	Completion Date	Notes
185	G. Forbes, Peterhead	11. 7.42	Jan 1946 Italy as DR215, 1951—108th MSS, 1954 Chatham, 21.11.56 sold Pounds Portsmouth.
186	R. Irvin, Peterhead	4. 5.42	Feb 1946 for sale.
187	R. Irvin, Peterhead	24. 7.42	25.8.55 sold for BU.
188	J. Noble, Fraserburgh	2. 6.42	25.8.55 sold for BU.
189	Wilson Noble, Fraserburgh	19. 8.42	1946-1950 Belgium, 25.8.55 sold.
190	J. & G. Forbes, Sandhaven	25. 4.42	1946—118th MSS, 1950 sold renamed 'STORMVOGEL'.
191	Macduff Eng & Ship Builders	6. 8.42	1947 Belgium, 1954 Chatham, 18.10.55 sold.
192	Herd & Mackenzie, Buckie	18. 5.42	April 1946 Salcombe. 1946 sold
193	Herd & Mackenzie, Buckie	14. 8.42	1946 Belgium, 1954 Chatham. 30. 1.57 sold for BU.
196	Clare Ship Building Co, Metaghan	15.12.42	1944—122nd MSS, 1946 sold
197	Clare Ship Building Co, Metaghan	15.12.42	Oct 1946 Burma R.N.V.R., Jan 1948 transferred to Burma.
198	Clare Ship Building Co, Metaghan	15.12.42	1946 sold at Shanghai.
199	Clare Ship Building Co, Metaghan	10. 2.43	March 1946 for sale.
200	Shelburne Co, Nova Scotia	24. 3.43	1946 sold at Shanghai.
201	Wagstaff & Hatfield, Canada	24. 3.43	Nov 1946 Burma R.N.V.R., Jan 1948 Transferred to Burma.
202	J.L. Bolson, Poole	8.42	1947 sold.
204	F. Curtis, Par	27. 9.42	1945-1947 France. 16. 2.48 sold.
205	F. Curtis, Par	27. 8.42	1946 sold.
206	J.S. Doig, Grimsby	17. 9.42	1945—144th MSS, Feb 1946 sold, renamed 'ALO'.
213	Humphrey & Smith, Grimsby	12. 9.42	1945-1947 France as D378, Oct 1947 for sale.
214	Macduff Eng & Shipbuilding Co.	12.11.42	Feb 1946 for sale, sold renamed 'PAX'.
217	W. Reekie, St Monance	13. 8.42	1949—1st MSS, 1951—50th MSS, 23.9.55 sold.
218	J.W. & A. Upham, Brixham	10.10.42	April, 1946 sold renamed 'ALVA 4'.
220	F. Curtis, Totnes	26. 8.42	1945-47 France as D373, Oct 1947 for sale at Portsmouth.
221	F. Curtis, Totnes	8.10.42	1945-47 France as D371, 5.3.48 sold.
222	Belmont Dock Co, Kingston, Jamaica	7.46	1946 Bermuda, 1947-51 renamed 'AMBER', 1955 sold.
223	Belmont Dock Co, Kingston, Jamaica	1.46	1946 Bermuda, June 1947 'MALABAR', Dec 1947 renamed 'JADE' 25.2.51 sank in storm off S.E. Jamaica.

MMS 217 (1717) July 1950

MMS	Builders	Completion Date	Notes
224	F. Curtis, Par	22.11.42	1945—117th MMS, 1946—109th MMS, 1947 Chatham, 1951 —104th MMS, 1952 Chatham, 22.4.54 sold as houseboat, Medway.
225	F. Curtis, Par	21.12.42	Jan 1946 sold renamed 'STANDARD II'.
228	F. Curtis, Par	8.11.42	1945—143rd MSS, & 117th MSS, 1946—102nd MMS, 1947 Chatham, Feb to July 1954 R.N.V.R. CURZON, 1954 Chatham, 20.2.57 sold mercantile.
233	J.L. Bolson, Poole	22.11.42	1945—132nd MMS, 1946—104th MSS, Feb 1948 to Nov 1954 R.N.V.R. ST DAVID, 1954 Chatham, 14.3.58 sold.
236	Wivenhoe Ship Yard Ltd	29.11.42	1945—116th MSS, 1946—102nd MMS, 1947 Portsmouth, 1952—51st MMS, 1954 Sheerness, 26.2.56 sold.

MMS 236 (March 1949)

MMS	Builders	Completion Date	Notes
238	Steers, St Johns,	17.11.43	1945—163rd MSS, Aug 1946 for sale.
239	Steers, St Johns, Newfoundland	17.11.43	1945-1946 159th MSS (Dutch) March 1950 sold.
240	Steers, St Johns, Newfoundland	13.12.43	1945—165th MSS, 20.1.47 sold.
241	Steers, St Johns, Newfoundland	13.12.43	1943 to 1946 163rd MMS, (ST BARBE) 3.47 — sold.
243	Clare Ship Bldg Co, Metaghan	12. 5.43	Feb 1946 — for sale.
245	Clare Ship Bldg Co, Metaghan	7. 6.43	Feb 1946 to Air Ministry as AIRMOOR 3, May 1946 for sale.
247	Clare Ship Bldg Co, Metaghan	29. 6.43	Jan 1946 to Air Ministry as AIRMOOR 1, April 1946 for sale.
249	Shelburne Co, Nova Scotia	—	Feb 1946 for sale.
250	Wagstaff & Hatfield, Canada	11.43	1946 sold renamed 'HARSTAD'
251	Wagstaff & Hatfield, Canada	30. 6.43	1946 sold renamed 'PROTECTOR III'.
252	Le Blanc Sh Bldg Co, Weymouth	7. 9.43	Jan 1946 for sale.
253	Le Blanc Sh Bldg Co,	7. 9.43	Feb 1946 for sale.
254	Chantiers Marit, St Laurent	23. 6.43	1945 Plymouth, Jan 1946 for sale.
255	Chantiers Marit, St Laurent	23. 6.43	1946 sold renamed 'FROMTIDEN'.
256	Vaughan, St Andrews, New Brunswick	43	Jan 1946 to Air Ministry as 'AIRMOOR 2', May 1946 for sale.
258	Rayal Bodden, Cayman Is.	3.46	March 1946 for sale.
259	Rayal Bodden, Cayman Is.	4.46	April 1946 for sale.
260	W. Reekie, St Monance	3. 4.43	1946 sold renamed 'ROFJELL'.
261	R. Irvin, Peterhead	24.11.42	1946—104th MMS, Feb 1948 to May, 1953 R.N.V.R. 'VENTURER', 1953 Chatham, 1954 Gibraltar, 3.1.57 sold.
263	Clapson & Sons, Barton-on-Humber	16. 1.43	1944 to 1948 Denmark, 1948 Chatham, 1952 Portsmouth, 23.9.55 sold.
265	F. Curtis, Totnes	16.11.42	Aug 1946 for sale.
266	F. Curtis, Totnes	13.12.42	1946—118th MMS (Belgium), 25.8.55 sold for BU.
267	F. Curtis, Totnes	28. 2.43	July 1946 sold renamed 'FRANKLYN'.
269	F. Curtis, Par	8. 3.43	1945—116th MMS, 3.1.47 sold renamed 'VIGDAR'.
270	F. Curtis, Par	24. 1.43	Nov 1945 sold renamed 'BOKNAFJELL'.
271	F. Curtis, Par	15. 2.43	1945—117th MMS, 1946—102nd MMS, 1947 Chatham, 1948—50th MMS, 1951—51st MMS, 1952 Rosyth, May 1958 BU at Inverkeithing.

MMS	Builders	Completion Date	Notes
272	J.W. & A. Upham, Brixham	26. 4.43	1946—101st MMS, 1947 Chatham, 1950—301st MMS, 1951—51st MMS, 1952 Chatham, 1954 Gibraltar, 3.1.57 sold.
274	J. Morris, Fareham	11. 5.43	May 1946 for sale.
275	Macduff Eng & Ship Bldg Co.	26. 7.43	1945—116th MMS, 1946— 109th MMS, 1947 Chatham, 1950 to 1954 'NEPTUNE', 21.3.55 sold - houseboat.
276	Macduff Eng & Ship Bldg Co.	27.12.43	July 1946 sold at Shanghai.
278	R. Irvin, Peterhead	8. 3.43	14.9.44 wrecked near St Malo, March 1946 abandoned.
279	W. Reekie, St Monance	23. 1.44	March 1946 sold renamed 'FRYDENLUND'.
280	Clapson & Sons,	29. 6.43	March 1946 sold renamed 'LAHELA 3'.
282	J.L. Bolson, Poole	10.43	May 1946 sold renamed 'BOMMELOY'.
283	J.W. & A. Upham, Brixham	18.10.43	1945—104th MMS, 1946 Chatham, 1951—104th MMS, 1953 Chatham, 21.3.57 sold for BU.
284	F. Curtis, Totnes	23. 3.43	Jan 1946 for sale.
285	F. Curtis, Par	28. 2.43	1946—101st MMS, 1947 Chatham, Dec 1950 to Jan 1954 R.N.V.R. ISIS, 21.1.55 sold as houseboat - Medway.
286	F. Curtis, Par	19. 4.43	1946—102nd MMS, 1947 Chatham, 1951—51st MMS, 1951 Hong Kong, 17.11.58 sold at Hong Kong.
287	J. Morris	20. 9.43	1945—116th MMS, May 1946 sold renamed 'GLOMFJOR'.
288	J. Morris	18. 7.43	1946—102nd MMS, 1948 Chatham, 1950—301st MMS, 1951—51st MMS, 21.10.52 foundered off Winterton Ness.
289	J. Morris	29.11.43	1945—116th MMS, 1946— 109th MMS, 1947 Chatham, May 1951 to Jan 1954 THAMES R.N.V.R., 1954 Chatham, 22.1.59 sold.
290	F. Curtis, Totnes	7. 8.43	1946—109th MMS, 1947 Chatham, 1951—104th MMS, 1953 Chatham, 22.2.55 sold.
291	F. Curtis, Totnes	17.10.43	1946—102nd MMS, 1947 Chatham, 1951—104th MMS, 1953 Chatham, 21.11.56 sold.
293	F. Curtis, Par	3. 6.43	1946—102nd MMS, 1947 DGV at Portsmouth, Nov 1950 sold.
294	F. Curtis, Par	31.5.43	1945—113th MMS, 1946— 104th MMS, 1947 Chatham, Sept 1952 sold.

MMS 1783 (283)

MMS	Builders	Completion Date	Notes
295	F. Curtis, Par	13. 6.43	As MMS 294, April 1946 for sale.
296	F. Curtis, Par	11. 7.43	1945—132nd MMS, 1946—109th MMS, 1947 Chatham, 1951—104th MMS, 1952 Chatham, 18.12.54 sold.
297	F. Curtis, Par	22. 8.43	1946—101st MMS, 1947 Chatham, 1952—120th MMS (Hong Kong), Nov 1958 sold at Hong Kong.
298	F. Curtis, Par	27. 9.43	Feb 1946 sold renamed 'PRODUSENT'.
300	Philip & Son, Dartmouth	31. 1.44	1946 sold at Shanghai.

An (unknown) MMS prepares for dry docking

MMS 1801 (301) June 1953

MMS	Builders	Completion Date	Notes
301	Wilson Noble, Fraserburgh	9. 8.43	1946—104th MMS, 1947 Chatham, 1950—301st MMS, 1951—51st MMS, 1954 Rosyth, 20.8.56 sold Pounds, Portsmouth.
302	R. Irvin, Peterhead	27. 6.43	April 1946 sold renamed 'OSLAND'.
303	J.W. & A. Upham, Brixham	12. 6.44	July 1946 sold at Shanghai.
304	J.L. Bolson, Poole	3. 4.44	July 1946 sold at Shanghai.
307	Wilson Noble, Fraserburgh	8.12.43	1944 to 1948 Denmark, 1949 Chatham, 1951—50th MMS, 1952 Portland, 1955 Chatham, 21.11.56 sold.
308	R. Irvin, Peterhead	6. 9.43	1945—113th MMS, Feb 1946 sold renamed 'ROYOY'.
309	Husband Yacht Yard, Marchwood	27. 9.43	1945—117th MMS, June 1946 for sale.
310	Abdul Wahbad, Beirut	1. 8.45	1945—146th MMS, June 1946 to Sept 1951 Greek 'ANDROS', 1951 Malta, 1952 Chatham, 18.10.55 sold.
311	Marine Trust, Tel Aviv	15. 1.45	1945—146th MMS, 1946 Malta, Jan 1947 sold.
312	Marine Trust, Tel Aviv	30. 1.45	1945—146th MMS, 1946 Malta, Feb 1947 sold.
313	Abdul Wahbad, Beirut	2.10.45	1945—146th MMS, April 1948 to Oct 1951 Greek 'SYROS', 1951 Malta, 17.10.55 sold at Malta.

M.M.S. 1001 Series

A need was soon seen for a larger, more modern version of the M.M.S. and this appeared in 1943-45 with the Admiralty type No's 1001-1090.

Displacement: 255 tons.
Dimensions: 126 (pp) 139¾ (oa) x 26 x 10½'.
Speed: 10 knots.
Armament: 2-20mm (2 x 1) guns.
Complement: 21.

1001 added to original numbers.

FLOTILLA SERVICE
(only those that saw service after 1945 are included)

101st Flotilla	— 1946-1947 Sheerness.
102nd "	— 1941-1947 Sheerness.
103rd "	— 1942-1946 Mediterranean.
104th "	— 1945-1946 Nore, 1951/53 Nore.
108th "	— 1942-1946, 1951-1953 Mediterranean.
109th "	— 1946-1947 North West Europe.
114th "	— 1942-1946 Mediterranean.
116th "	— 1945-1946 North West Europe.
117th "	— 1945-1947 North West Europe.
118th "	— 1943-1947 North West Europe.
120th "	— 1942-1946 Mediterranean/Persian Gulf.
122nd "	— 1944-1947 East Indies.
135th "	— 1944-1946 Portsmouth.
139th Dutch	— 1945-1947 Dutch Waters.
146th "	— 1945-1946 Levant.
202nd "	— 1946 North West Europe.
204th "	— 1945-1946 North Shields.
205th "	— 1946 Lowestoft.
159th Flotilla	— 1944-1946 Normandy Invasion Force/NW Europe.
165th "	— 1946 Harwich.
50th "	— 1951-1952 Port Edgar.
51st "	— 1951-1954 Port Edgar.
52nd "	— 1950-1951 Port Edgar.

MMS	Builders	Completion Date	Notes
1001	Camper & Nicholsons, Gosport	26. 7.43	1946 sold.
1002	Camper & Nicholsons, Gosport	24. 1.44	1946 Sheerness, 1947 Devonport, 1950 D.G.V. 400, 24.1.73 BU.
1003	Wivenhoe Shipyard, Southampton	22. 9.43	1947 Chatham, 1950 D.G.V. 401. 1950 Rosyth, 11.4.68 sold.
1004	Wivenhoe Shipyard, Southampton	20. 1.44	1947 Chatham, 1950 D.G.V. 402, 1952 Singapore, 1.61 sold.
1006	Richards Ironworks, Lowestoft	22. 3.43	20.1.47 sold renamed 'TRIPPESTA'.
1007	E. Anglian Constructors, Oulton Broad.	21. 6.43	1946 Sheerness, 5.5.47 sold.
1008	E. Anglian Constructors, Oulton Broad.	21. .43	3.3.47 sold.
1009	Wivenhoe Shipyard, Milford Haven	28. 2.43	24.1.47 sold.
1010	Wivenhoe Shipyard, Milford Haven	21. 6.43	11.11.46 sold.
1011	Wivenhoe Shipyard, Milford Haven	28. 8.43	1946 Chatham, 1950 D.G.V. 403. 1950 Portsmouth, 20.5.68 sold.
1012	Wivenhoe Shipyard, Milford Haven	15.10.43	10.46 sold. Renamed 'PRESTIGE'. 2.7.53. Repurchased for D.G.V. 404. 1953 Chatham. 22.10.58 sold for BU.
1013	G. Forbes, Peterhead	25.5.43	9.12.46 sold, renamed 'UDDU'.
1014	P.K. Harris, Appledore	29. 6.43	1944-45—203rd MMS. 1952 BU.
1015	Herd & Mackenzie, Buckie	7. 6.43	25.10.46 sold.
1016	Herd & Mackenzie, Buckie	29. 9.43	7.8.45 Danish Navy, 29.1.46 wrecked Jutland.
1017	J. & G. Forbes, Sandhaven	15. 1.43	1946—206th, 1946 Sheerness 9.47 to 2.54 R.N.V.R. 'CURZON'. 22.12.58 BU.
1018	W. Reekie, Anstruther	7. 7.43	4.10.46 sold.
1020	J.W. & A. Upham, Brixham	14. 2.44	7.46 Belgium (118th) to 10.48. 25.8.55 sold.
1021	J. Noble, Fraserburgh	9. 4.43	4.11.46 sold.
1024	J. & G. Forbes, Sandhaven	12. 7.43	1.46 to 10.47 France as D343. 18.3.48 sold.
1026	J.S. Doig, Grimsby	7. 6.43	2.52 to Indonesia.
1027	E. Anglian Constructors, Oulton Broad	15.12.43	22.11.46 sold, renamed 'SOLNES'.
1028	J.W. & A. Upham, Brixham	17. 1.44	1945-208th. 1946 sold.
1029	J.W. & A. Upham, Brixham	5. 3.45	1945—208th, 1946 Dover. 1946 Salcombe. 5.46 not listed.
1030	Philip & Son, Dartmouth	25.10.43	1946—202nd, 1946 Sheerness, 8.47 R.N.V.R. Hull, 2.48 to 12.54 HUMBER, 1954 Chatham, 22.1.59 sold.

MMS	Builders	Completion Date	Notes
1031	P.K. Harris, Appledore	10.11.43	1946 sold.
1032	F. Curtis, Par	27.8.43	1.46 to 10.47 French as D342. 4.4.51 sold.
1033	F. Curtis, Par	8.11.43	1.46 to 10.47 French as D345. 23.2.48 sold.
1034	F. Curtis, Par	26.6.44	1946 Sheerness, 1.47 R.N.V.R. Belfast, 2.48 to 2.54 'KILMOREY', 12.55 sold.
1035	F. Curtis, Totnes	18. 7.43	1.46 to 2.46 French Navy. 1948 Portsmouth 15.3.54 sold.
1036	F. Curtis, Totnes	15.11.43	1.46 to 1.47 French as D346. 2.4.51 sold.
1037	Richards Ironworks, Lowestoft	27. 4.43	20.1.47 sold, renamed 'TRAPPES'. 26.2.49 foundered.
1038	Richards Ironworks, Lowestoft	25. 8.43	8.45 to 11.50 Danish Navy. 1951 Chatham. 1951—51st M/S. 1945 Rosyth. 1956 Chatham. 19.1.59 sold.
1039	Wivenhoe Shipyard, Milford Haven	26. 9.44	1946 to 10.47 French Navy as D341. 7.7.48 sold.
1040	F. Curtis, Par	28. 4.44	1946 to 1947 French Navy as D344. 18.2.48 sold.
1041	W. Reekie, Anstruther	8. 2.44	18.10.46 sold.
1042	Humphrey & Smith, Grimsby	9.43	6.45 to 11.50 Danish Navy, 1950 Chatham, 1952 Portsmouth, 1954 Chatham, 19.3.57 sold.
1043	Humphrey & Smith, Grimsby	9.43	1945—203rd M/S. 1952 BU.
1044	Wivenhoe Shipyard,	2. 8.44	6.45 to 11.50 Danish Navy. 1950 Chatham. 1952 Portsmouth. 1953 Chatham. 25.11.54 sold.
1045	G. Forbes, Peterhead	19.10.43	1945—208th M/S. 1.3.48 sold.
1046	E. Anglian Constructors, Oulton Broad	3.44	1945—203rd M/S. 1952 BU.
1047	Herd & Mackenzie, Buckie	17. 1.44	22.11.46 sold.
1048	J. Noble, Frazerburgh	22. 9.43	1946 Sheerness. 9.47 R.N.V.R. Clyde. 2.48 to 10.50 'GRAHAM'. 5.7.57 sold.
1049	J. & G. Forbes, Sandhaven	4.11.43	1946 sold.
1050	Clare Shipbuilding Co, Metaghan	14. 6.44	23.7.46 sold renamed 'ELIESOR'.
1051	Clare Shipbuilding Co, Metaghan	18. 7.44	1946 sold renamed 'TIMANN'.
1052	Clare Shipbuilding Co, Metaghan	24. 8.44	1946 sold renamed 'ARCUS'.
1053	Clare Shipbuilding Co, Metaghan	25. 9.44	1946 sold renamed 'THOR-BJORN'.
1054	Clare Shipbuilding Co, Metaghan	21.11.44	1945—209th M/S. 2.45 to 12.45 French Navy as D345. 1946 sold renamed 'DOLPHIN'.
1055	Clare Shipbuilding Co, Metaghan	21.11.44	1945—209th M/S. 5.45 to .46 French Navy as D344. 1946 sold renamed 'HAVBRANT'.

(Unknown) MMS; 1001 Series

73

MMS	Builders	Completion Date	Notes
1056	Clare Shipbuilding Co, Metaghan	11. 1.45	1945 Plymouth. 28.6.46 sold renamed 'JANE LOLK'.
1057	Clare Shipbuilding Co, Metaghan	11. 1.45	1945—208th M/S. 3.46 sold.
1058	Clare Shipbuilding Co, Metaghan	26. 2.45	1945—208th M/S. 5.46 sold renamed 'JORGEN CLAUS'.
1059	Clare Shipbuilding Co, Metaghan	27. 3.45	1945 North Shields, 5.46 for sale.
1060	Clare Shipbuilding Co, Metaghan	2. 5.45	1945 North Shields. 1945—60th M/S Port Edgar. 1947 Rosyth. 3.53 to 8.54 R.N.V.R. 'ST MUNGO'. 1954 Chatham. 12.1.58 sold.
1061	Clare Shipbuilding Co, Metaghan	2. 6.45	1945 North Shields, 1945—60th M/S. 1947 Training-Port Edgar. 1950—301st M/S. 1951 Chatham. 3.54 to 9.54 R.N.V.R. 'MERSEY'. 30.7.57 sold Pounds, Portsmouth for BU.
1062	Wagstaff & Hatfield, Canada	16.5.44	1946 sold.
1063	Wagstaff & Hatfield, Canada	15. 6.44	1946 sold.
1064	Wagstaff & Hatfield, Canada	24. 8.44	1946 sold, renamed 'KROHNOY'.
1065	Wagstaff & Hatfield, Canada	22.11.44	6.45 to 1946. French Navy as D343. 3.46 for sale.
1066	Wagstaff & Hatfield, Canada	10. 3.45	1946 sold renamed 'LADY PATRICIA'.
1067	Wagstaff & Hatfield, Canada	27. 2.45	1945 North Shields. 5.46 for sale.
1068	Vaughan, St Andrews, New Brunswick	17. 7.44	3.46 for sale.
1069	Vaughan, St Andrews, New Brunswick	23. 9.44	5.45 to 12.45 French Navy as D341. 1946 sold.
1070	Vaughan, St Andrews, New Brunswick	25.10.44	5.45 to 12.45 French Navy as D345. 3.46 for sale.
1075	F. Curtis, Totnes	25. 2.44	1946 Sheerness. 2.48 to 3.54 R.N.V.R. 'MERSEY'. 1954 Chatham. 25.2.58 sold.
1076	F. Curtis, Totnes	1. 7.44	27.1.47 sold, renamed 'FENMORE'
1077	F. Curtis, Looe	4.11.44	1946 Chatham. 2.48 to 1.55 R.N.V.R. 'MONTROSE'. 1955 Chatham. 20.7.56 sold Pounds, Portsmouth for BU.
1078	F. Curtis, Par	3. 3.45	1945—208th M/S. 1946 Dover. 1946 Salcombe. 5.46 not listed.
1079	F. Curtis, Par	45	1946 Dan Layer, Dover. 11.46 for sale.
1080	F. Curtis, Par	45	1945 Dan Layer, Humber. 1946 Dover. 1946 Sheerness. 11.46 sold, renamed 'BENN'.
1081	J.S Doig, Grimsby	8.11.43	27.5.46 sold for Mercantile use.

MMS	Builders	Completion Date	Notes
1083	Wivenhoe Ship Yard Ltd	6.10.44	1945—208th M/S. 1946 Sheerness. 1946 Salcombe. 1946 sold.
1084	Wivenhoe Ship Yard Ltd	5. 3.45	1945—117th M/S. 1946 sold, renamed 'ADMIRAL HAWKINS'.
1087	F. Curtis	22. 6.45	1945—208th M/S. 1946 Plymouth. 1946 Salcombe. 4.46 not listed.
1088	F. Curtis, Totnes	45	1946 sold. Renamed 'SVEIP'.
1089	East Anglian Constructors, Oulton Broad	8. 3.45	1945—206th M/S. 1947 Sheerness. 1948 R.N.V.R. 'FORTH'. 8.51 to 9.54 RNVR 'KILLIECRANKIE'. 1954 Chatham. 19.3.57 sold, renamed 'LARACHE'.
1090	Philip & Sons, Dartmouth	29. 1.45	1945—206th M/S. 1947 Sheerness. 2.48 R.N.V.R. 'COQUET'. 9.48 R.N.V.R. 'BERNICIA'. 7.54 to 10.54 R.N.V.R. 'NORTHUMBRIA'. 1954 Chatham. 1958 sold.

TON CLASS

Displacement:	360 tons (Standard) 440 tons (Full load).
Dimensions:	153' x 27.7' x 8.2'
Armament:	Ships vary, some sweepers having no 40mm, some 1-40mm and 2-20mm, whilst Hunters have 1-40mm.
Main Engines:	2 diesels; 2 shafts; 2500 bhp.
Speed:	15 knots.
Oil Fuel:	45 tons.
Range, Miles:	2,500 at 12 knots.
Complement:	29. 38 in minehunters. (5 officers & 33 ratings).

Name	PT No	Completed	Builders
ALCASTON	M.1102	16.12.53	J.I. Thornycroft, Southampton
ALDINGTON (ex PITTINGTON)	M.1171	18. 4.56	Camper & Nicholson Ltd., Southampton
ALFRISTON	M.1103	16. 3.54	J.I. Thornycroft, Southampton
ALVERTON	M.1104	24. 3.54	Camper & Nicholson Ltd, Southampton
AMERTON	M.1105	17. 7.54	Camper & Nicholson Ltd, Southampton
APPLETON	M.1106	18. 3.54	Goole Shipbuilding Co. Ltd.
ASHTON	M.1198	15. 4.58	White's Shipyard Ltd, Southampton
BADMINTON (ex ILSTON)	M.1149	5. 7.55	Camper & Nicholson Ltd, Gosport
BEACHAMPTON	M.1107	30. 7.54	Goole Shipbuilding Co. Ltd.
BELTON	M.1199	31. 5.57	J.S. Doige, (Grimsby) Ltd.
BEVINGTON	M.1108	9. 3.54	White's Shipyard Ltd, Southampton
BICKINGTON	M.1109	25. 5.54	White's Shipyard Ltd, Southampton
BILDESTON	M.1110	28. 4.53	J.S. Doige (Grimsby) Ltd
BLAXTON	M.1132	24. 4.56	J.I. Thornycroft, Southampton
BOSSINGTON (ex EMBLETON)	M.1133	11.12.56	J.I. Thornycroft, Southampton
BOULSTON	M.1112	29. 4.54	Richards, Lowestoft
BRERETON	M.1113	9. 7.54	Richards, Lowestoft
BRINTON	M.1114	4. 3.54	Cook, Welton & Gemmell Ltd, Beverley
BRONINGTON	M.1115	4. 6.54	Cook, Welton & Gemmell Ltd, Beverley
BURNASTON	M.1116	3. 3.54	Fleetlands, Shipyards Ltd, Gosport
BUTTINGTON	M.1117	5. 6.54	Fleetlands, Shipyards Ltd, Gosport
CALTON	M.1118	12.11.54	Wivenhoe Shipyard Ltd
CARHAMPTON	M.1119	30. 5.56	Wivenhoe Shipyard Ltd
CASTLETON	M.1207	11.11.58	White's Shipyard Ltd, Southampton
CAUNTON	M.1120	2. 4.54	Montrose Shipyard Ltd
CHAWTON	M.1209	23. 7.58	Fleetlands Shipyards Ltd, Gosport
CHEDISTON	M.1121	28. 9.54	Montrose Shipyard Ltd
CHILCOMPTON	M.1122	8.10.54	Herd & Mackenzie, Buckie, Banff
CHILTON	M.1215	58	Cook, Welton & Gemmell Ltd, Beverley
CLARBESTON	M.1123	2. 1.55	Richards, Lowestoft
CRICHTON (ex OSSINGTON)	M.1124	23. 4.54	J.S. Doige (Grimsby) Ltd
CONISTON	M.1101	17. 5.53	J.I. Thornycroft, Southampton
CROFTON	M.1216	22. 8.58	J.I. Thornycroft, Southampton
CUXTON	M.1125	13.10.54	Camper & Nicholson Ltd, Southampton
DALSWINTON	M.1126	19.10.54	White's Shipyard Ltd, Southampton
DARLASTON	M.1127	5.10.54	Cook, Welton & Gemmel Ltd, Berverley
DARTINGTON	M.1203	26. 6.58	Philip & Son, Dartmouth
DERRITON	M.1128	1. 6.54	J.I. Thornycroft, Southampton

Name	PT No	Completed	Builders
DILSTON	M.1168	20. 7.55	Cook, Welton & Gemmell Ltd, Beverley
DUFTON	M.1145	29. 7.55	Goole Shipbuilders + Eng. Co. Ltd
DUMBLETON	M.1212	10. 7.58	Harland & Wolff, Belfast
DUNKERTON	M.1144	24. 3.55	Goole Shipbuilders + Eng. Co. Ltd
DURWESTON	M.1201	17. 8.56	Dorset Yacht Co. Poole
EDDERTON	M.1111	10. 3.54	J.S. Doige (Grimsby) Ltd
ESSINGTON	M.1134	18. 5.55	Camper & Nicholson Ltd, Southampton
FENTON	M.1135	16. 8.55	Camper & Nicholson Ltd, Southampton
FISKERTON	M.1206	18. 4.58	J.S. Doige (Grimsby) Ltd
FITTLETON	M.1136	28. 1.55	White's Shipyard Ltd, Southampton
FLOCKTON	M.1137	7.10.55	White's Shipyard Ltd, Southampton
FLORISTON	M.1138	19. 8.55	Richards, Ironworks Ltd Lowestoft
GAVINTON	M.1140	14. 7.54	J.S. Doige (Grimsby) Ltd
GLASSERTON	M.1141	31.12.54	J.S. Doige (Grimsby) Ltd
HAZELTON	M.1142	2. 3.55	Cook, Welton & Gemmell Ltd, Beverley
HEXTON	M.1143	2.11.55	Cook, Welton & Gemmell Ltd, Beverley
HICKLETON	M.1131	24. 6.55	J.I. Thornycroft, Southampton
HIGHBURTON	M.1130	8. 6.55	J.I. Thornycroft, Southampton
HODGESTON	M.1146	17.12.54	Fleetlands Shipyard Ltd, Gosport
HOUGHTON	M.1211	6. 6.58	Camper & Nicholson Ltd, Gosport
HUBBERSTON	M.1147	14.10.55	Fleetlands Shipyard, Gosport
ILMINGTON	M.1148	5. 1.55	Camper & Nicholson Ltd, Gosport
INVERMORISTON	M.1150	20. 1.55	Dorset Yacht Co. Poole
IVESTON	M.1151	29. 6.55	Philip & Son, Dartmouth
JACKTON	M.1152	20. 7.56	Philip & Son, Dartmouth
KEDLESTON	M.1153	2. 7.55	Wm Pickersgill, Sunderland
KELLINGTON	M.1154	4.11.55	Wm Pickersgill, Sunderland
KEMERTON	M.1156	21. 5.54	Harland & Wolff, Belfast
KILDARTON (ex LISTON)	M.1162	25.11.55	Harland & Wolff, Belfast
·KIRKLISTON	M.1157	21. 8.54	Harland & Wolff, Belfast
LALESTON	M.1158	10.11.54	Harland & Wolff, Belfast
LANTON	M.1159	10. 3.55	Harland & Wolff, Belfast
LETTERSTON	M.1160	29. 6.55	Harland & Wolff, Belfast
LEVERTON	M.1161	25. 8.55	Harland & Wolff, Belfast
LEWISTON	M.1208	16. 6.60	Herd & Mackenzie, Buckie, Banff
LULLINGTON	M.1163	1. 6.56	Harland & Wolff, Belfast
MADDISTON	M.1164	8.11.56	Harland & Wolff, Belfast
MAXTON	M.1165	19. 2.57	Harland & Wolff, Belfast
MARYTON	M.1202	13.11.58	Montrose Shipyard
MONKTON (ex KELTON)	M.1155	27. 2.57	Herd & Mackenzie, Buckie, Banff
NURTON	M.1166	21. 8.57	Harland & Wolff, Belfast
OAKINGTON	M.1213	11. 2.59	Harland & Wolff, Belfast
OULSTON	M.1129	19. 7.55	J.I. Thornycroft, Southampton
OVERTON	M.1197	28. 8.56	Camper & Nicholson, Gosport
PACKINGTON	M.1214	21. 5.59	Harland & Wolff, Belfast
PENSTON	M.1169	9. 3.56	Cook, Welton & Gemmell Ltd, Beverley
PICKTON	M.1170	19. 7.56	Cook, Welton & Gemmell Ltd, Beverley
POLLINGTON	M.1173	5. 9.58	Camper & Nicholson, Southampton
PUNCHESTON	M.1174	20. 9.57	Richards Ironworks, Lowestoft
QUAINTON	M.1175	5. 2.59	Richards Ironworks, Lowestoft
RENNINGTON	M.1176	27. 4.60	Richards Ironworks, Lowestoft
REPTON (ex OSSINGTON)	M.1167	12.12.57	Harland & Wolff, Belfast
RODDINGTON	M.1177	22. 7.55	Fleetlands Shipyard, Gosport
SANTON	M.1178	21. 2.56	Fleetlands Shipyard, Gosport

Name	PT No	Completed	Builders
SEFTON	M.1179	28. 6.55	White's Shipyard Ltd, Southampton
SHAVINGTON	M.1180	1. 3.56	White's Shipyard Ltd, Southampton
SHERATON	M.1181	24. 8.56	White's Shipyard Ltd, Southampton
SHOULTON	M.1182	16.11.55	Montrose Shipyard
SINGLETON	M.1183	25. 9.56	Montrose Shipyard
SOBERTON	M.1200	17. 9.57	Fleetlands Shipyards Ltd, Gosport
SOMERLEYTON (ex GAMSTON)	M.1139	31. 8.56	Richards Ironworks, Lowestoft
STRATTON	M.1210	7. 1.59	Dorset Yacht Co., Poole
STUBBINGTON	M.1204	30. 7.57	Camper & Nicholson Ltd, Gosport
SULLINGTON	M.1184	23. 3.55	J.S. Doige (Grimsby) Ltd.
SWANSTON	M.1185	27. 7.55	J.S. Doige (Grimsby) Ltd.
TARLTON	M.1186	14.12.55	J.S. Doige (Grimsby) Ltd.
THANKERTON	M.1172	10. 5.57	Camper & Nicholson Ltd, Southampton
UPTON	M.1187	25. 7.56	J.I. Thornycroft & Co, Southampton
WALKERTON	M.1188	10. 1.58	J.I. Thornycroft & Co, Southampton
WASPERTON	M.1189	19. 7.57	White's Shipyard Ltd, Southampton
WENNINGTON	M.1190	30. 8.56	J.S. Doige (Grimsby) Ltd.
WHITTON	M.1191	21. 8.56	Fleetlands Shipyard Ltd, Gosport
WILTON	M.1116	12. 6.73	Vosper Thornycroft Ltd, Woolston
WILKIESTON	M.1192	24. 7.57	Cook, Welton & Gemmell Ltd, Beverley
WISTON	M.1205	17. 2.60	Winvenhoe Shipyard
WOLVERTON	M.1193	25. 3.58	Montrose Shipyard
WOOLASTON	M.1194	10.10.58	Herd & Mackenzie, Buckie
WOTTON	M.1195	13. 6.57	Philip & Son, Dartmouth
YARNTON	M.1196	16. 1.57	Wm. Pickersgill & Sons Ltd, Sunderland

Name	Dates	Notes
ALCASTON	1953-54	Senior Officer 104th M.S.S.
	11.56	Operation Musketeer (Anglo/French Invasion of Suez Canal.)
	1961	Refit — Conversion to Deltic Engines, fitted with air conditioning and stabilisers
	21. 8.62	Commissioned and renamed H.M.A.S. 'Snipe'
	1.10.62	Sailed for Australia from Portsmouth
	4.69-12.70	Conversion to minehunter
ALDINGTON	1956-58	108th M.S.S.
	8.63	Sold to Ghana — renamed 'EJURA'
ALFRISTON	5.54	Renamed 'WARSASH' for R.N.R. Solent
	7.60	Renamed 'KILMOREY' for R.N.R. Ulster
	3. 3.76	Renamed ALFRISTON for FPS
	28. 6.77	Fleet Review at Spithead (F.P.S.)
	21.12.78	Rejoined 10th MCMS Solent Division R.N.R.
ALVERTON	6.54-2.62	London Division R.N.R. as 'THAMES'
	1967	Towed from Singapore to Gibraltar (with BLAXTON) by tug Samsonia
	22. 2.71	(At Gibraltar) Sold to Ireland — renamed 'BANBA'
AMERTON	1954-11.59	R.N.R. as 'MERSEY'
	1960-71	R.N.R. as 'CLYDE'
	1971	B.U. at Bo'ness
APPLETON	1954	Reserve
	11.56	Senior Officer 105th M.S.S. Operation Musketeer
	1957	100th M.S.S.
	3.62	Senior Officer 9th M.S.S. Based at Bahrein
	3.68	Sailed from Middle East for U.K.
	11.72	Arrived Neath for B.U. by Steel Co., (Western) Ltd

HMS Appleton (1956)

HMS Alfriston at Lisbon

ASHTON	7.58	108th M.S.S.
	1962	7th M.S.S. Mediterranean
	15. 1.68	Earthquake relief Sicilly
	31. 3.69	Sailed from Malta for Reserve at Gibraltar
	1972	Fishery Protection Squadron
	3.75	For disposal
	3. 8.77	Towed from Rosyth for B.U. at Blyth
BADMINTON	4.54-7.55	5th M.S.S.
	1955/56	108th M.S.S. Med.
	3.68	For disposal
	24. 4.70	Sold for B.U. to Rugg & Co. Ltd., London on behalf of Jacques Bakker & Zonen, Bruges, Belgium

HMS Badminton

HMS Beachampton as Hong Kong Patrol vessel.

Name	Dates	Notes
BEACHAMPTON	1958-8.64	5th M.S.S. H.M.S. 'VERNON'
	6. 1.65	Refitting at H.M. Dockyard Portsmouth
	4. 9.65	Sailed from U.K. for duties with 9th M.S.S. Persian Gulf
	9. 8.71	Sailed from Persian Gulf for Hong Kong
	17. 9.71	Arrived Hong Kong from Persian Gulf
	1971	Refitted and re-designated as Patrol Craft for duty with 6th Patrol Craft Squadron Hong Kong (P1007)

HMS Belton (note searchlight in lieu of 20mm)

BELTON	1958	Fishery Protection Squadron
	5.68	Operation 'Clear Road'
	8.68	Operation 'New Broom'
	10.71	Ran aground in the Hebrides, later refloated and taken to Greenock but found to be beyond repair. She was replaced by 'CHAWTON'
	25.11.74	Sold for B.U. Davies & Newman Ltd., London on behalf of M.H. Gonzalez of Gijon, Spain

Name	Dates	Notes
BEVINGTON	1954-55	104th M.S.S.
	1956	Operational Reserve at Hythe
	1967	Laid up at Hythe
		Sold to Argentina renamed 'TIERRA DE FUEGO' (M.4)
	1968	Refitted and modernised by Vosper Thornycroft fitted with activated fin stabiliser equipment
BICKINGTON	30.10.54	Renamed 'CURZON' Sussex Division R.N.R.
	1960	Renamed 'KILLIECRANKIE' Forth Division R.N.R.
	3.74	Extended Refit at Chatham
	1.76	Fishery Protection Squadron
	1982-83	F.P.S.
BILDESTON	1954-57	50th M.S.S.
	1.11.68	Commissioned as Minehunter at Rosyth on completion of 2½ years refit, 1st M.C.M.S.
	7.69	At Torbay, Western Fleet Review
	28. 6.77	Spithead Fleet Review (1st M.C.M.S.)
	1.80-1.81	STANAVFORCHAN
	81/83	1st M.C.M.S.
	1.1.84	3rd M.C.M.S.

HMS Bildeston. The first to be completed . . . May1953—the 'original' look. This ship was still in service 30 years later.

BLAXTON	11.56	105th M.S.S. Operation Musketeer
	1967	Towed from Singapore to Gibraltar (with ALVERTON) by tug Samsonia
	22. 2.72	(At Gibraltar) Sold to Ireland. Renamed FOLA (CM12)

Name	Dates	Notes
BOSSINGTON	58/59	Vernon Squadron (5th M.S.S.)
	7.63	5th M.S.S. Operation 'Cable Way'
	7.64	Converted to Minehunter at Chatham
	9.65	6th M.S.S. Far East
	6.10.69	Sailed from Singapore to Hong Kong
	1.10.71	Sailed from Hong Kong with 'HUBBERSTON' for U.K. Whilst on passage went to the assistance of H.M.S. 'ZULU' off the mouth of River Gambia. Towed 'ZULU' to Dakar.
	3. 1.72	2nd M.C.M.S. at Portsmouth
	5.73-12.73	Attached to STANAVFORCHAN
	7.4-1.10.74	Operation 'Rheostat' (Suez Canal)
	19. 9.75	Recommissioned at Gibraltar
	10.75	Arrived Portsmouth — 2nd M.C.M.S.
	6.76-12.76	Attached to STANAVFORCHAN
	28. 6.77	At Spithead Fleet Review 2nd M.C.M.S.
	1.78-9.78	STANAVFORCHAN
	23.6.82-83	2nd M.C.M.S.

HMS Bossington (8.9.58)

HMS Bossington
Ten years later . . . As a Minehunter. Note Armament.

Name	Dates	Notes
BOULSTON	1954	104th M.S.S.
	1956-57	50th M.S.S.
	3.60-69	H.M.S. 'WARSASH'. Solent Division R.N.R.
	11.75	Towed to Hayle for B.U. by Stanley Ferry Dismantlers Ltd.
BRERETON	11.54-61	'ST. DAVID' South Wales Division R.N.R.
	1965	F.P.S. Replaced H.M.S. 'SQUIRREL'
	1967	Conversion to Minehunter at Portsmouth
	1968	9th M.S.S. Persian Gulf
	12.71	Arrived Portsmouth from Persian Gulf
	1972	F.P.S. Replaced 'WASPERTON'
	12. 2.76	In collision with Danish fishing vessel off Hartlepool, holed below water line and taken in tow by R.M.A.S. 'KINLOSS'
	23. 6.82.	10th M.C.M.S. Mersey Division R.N.R.
BRINTON	1954-56	104th M.S.S.
	1956	Reserve (Admin by S.O.R.F. Chatham)
	6.64	3rd M.S.S.
	1968	Conversion to Minehunter at Devonport
	9.68	9th M.C.M.S. Persian Gulf
	12.71	Arrived Portsmouth from Persian Gulf — joined F.P.S. replaced 'WOTTON'
	26. 4.76	Recommissioned (FPS) after long refit at Chatham Dockyard
	28. 6.77	Spithead, Fleet Review
	7.81-9.81	STANAVFORCHAN
	23. 6.82	1st M.C.M.S.
	1.1.84	3rd M.C.M.S.

HMS Bronington

Name	Dates	Notes
BRONINGTON	1954	Renamed H.M.S. 'HUMBER' 10th M.S.S. R.N.R.
	1958	Commissioned again as BRONINGTON
	3.60	100th M.S.S.
	1.10.62	1st Minehunting Squadron, Port Edgar
	1965	Conversion to Minehunter at Rosyth
	5. 1.66	1st M.C.M.S.
	25. 5.68	Operation 'New Broom'
	15. 2.74	Sailed from Port Edgar for refit at Gibraltar
	1976	1st M.C.M.S. Rosyth
	9. 2.76	Lt. The Prince of Wales in Command
	14.11.77	H.M. Queen and Prince Phillip visited ship whilst at Tower Pier, London
	1980-84	2nd M.C.M.S. (7-12/83 STANAVFORCHAN)

HMS Burnaston

Name	Dates	Notes
BURNASTON	1954	104th M.S.S.
	1956	Reserve (Admin by S.O.R.F. Chatham)
	1957	100th M.S.S.
	18.10.59	108th M.S.S. Mediterranean. Stopped Turkish vessel 'DENIZ' off Cyprus and whilst boarding party were on board searching the vessel, the crew of 'DENIZ' scuttled their ship. Two cases of ammunition were salvaged before the vessel sank.
	12.64	Refitting at Portsmouth
	23. 8.65	Sailed from Portsmouth for Middle East to join 9th M.S.S. based at Bahrein.
	1969	Returned to UK
	13. 4.71	Sold to Metal Recoveries Ltd., Newhaven, Sussex for B.U.
BUTTINGTON	20.9.54	H.M.S. 'VENTURER' Severn Division R.N.R.
	2.62-69	H.M.S. 'THAMES' London Division R.N.R.
	3.70	For disposal
	1. 6.70	Sold for B.U. to Metal Recoveries (Newhaven)

HMS Calton (Apr '66)

Name	Dates	Notes
CALTON	1956	Refitting Sheerness
	4.66	9th M/S Persian Gulf — During her tour of duty she intercepted some 600 vessels off Aden, captured 4 Dhows heavily loaded with weapons which were being smuggled into the Country.
	14. 8.66	Arrived Portsmouth
	3.67	For disposal
	2. 7.68	Sold to C.H. Rugg, Belgium for B.U.
CARHAMPTON	1956	Operational Reserve at Hythe
	1956	104th M.S.S. Malta
	8.58	Aden
	9.65-8.66	9th M.S.S. Persian Gulf
	3.69	For disposal
	1. 7.70	Sold to H.K. Vickers & Son (Eng) Ltd., Sheffield and B.U. at Plymouth
CASTLETON	1959	Sold to South Africa — renamed 'JOHANNESBURG'
CAUNTON	14. 8.56	Vernon Squadron
	3.68	For disposal
	24. 4.70	Sold for B.U. to Metal Recoveries (Newhaven) Ltd

HMS Chawton - farewell to Singapore.

Name	Dates	Notes
CHAWTON	10.58	104th M.S.S. Malta
	21.10.59	Sailed from Malta to Singapore via Aden, Bombay and Colombo for 104th M.S.S.
	62-65	6th M.S.S.
	9.65-3.69	9th M.S.S.
	1971-74	Fishery Protection Squadron — replaced 'BELTON'
	3.75	For disposal
	6. 8.77	Arrived Tees for B.U. by Tees Marine, Middlesborough
CHEDISTON	1954-57	H.M.S. 'MONTROSE', Tay Division R.N.R.
	1961	Refitted for Australian Navy. Conversion to Deltic Engines. Fitted with air conditioning and stabilisers
	7. 9.62	Commissioned and renamed H.M.A.S. 'CURLEW'
	1.10.62	Sailed from Portsmouth to Australia
	67/68	Conversion to Minehunter
CHILCOMPTON	1954/62	Operational Reserve at Hythe
	5.62-9.65	9th M.S.S. Persian Gulf
	4.67-1.69	Fishery Protection Squadron
	3.70	For disposal
	16.11.71	Sold to Pounds Shipbreakers Havant, Hants
CHILTON	27.10.58	Transferred to South Africa at Hythe
	11.58	Sailed to South Africa as 'EAST LONDON'

Name	Dates	Notes
CLARBESTON	1955/57	104th M.S.S.
	1957-62	Operational Reserve Hythe
	3.62	Commissioned as replacement for Highburton (50th M.S.S.)
	4.3.63	Returned to Reserve fleet
	7.64-12.65	5th M.S.S.
	1966-68	3rd M.C.M.S.
	19. 3.67	Sailed from Plymouth for oil spraying operations after 'TORREY CANYON' going aground on Seven Stones
	3.68	Salvage operations with 'INVERMORISTON' and 'SHOULTON' off Rosslare after an Aer Lingus Viscount crashed on 24.3.68
	1. 7.70	Sold to H.K. Vickers & Sons, (Eng) Ltd., Sheffield B.U. at Plymouth

HMS Clarbeston 'sweeping.

Name	Dates	Notes
CRICHTON	1954-61	H.M.S. 'CLYDE' Mersey Division R.N.R.
	1961-76	H.M.S. 'ST. DAVID', South Wales Division R.N.R.
	1. 1.76	10th M.C.M.S. North West Group R.N.R.
	1977	Fishery Protection Squadron
	1981	1st M.C.M.S.
	23. 6.82	Fishery Protection Squadron

Early Days - HMS Coniston

Name	Dates	Notes
CONISTON	1954-57	104th M.S.S.
	1957-59	100th M.S.S.
	60/61	Operational Reserve Chatham
	2/62	Towed to Hythe
	4/62	Towed to Gibraltar (Reserve)
	63-70	Gibraltar and Hythe Reserve
	5. 2.70	Sold to Metal Recoveries (Newhaven) Ltd., for B.U.
CROFTON	10.58	108th M.S.S.
	1963	7th M.S.S. Mediterranean
	15. 1.68	7th M.S.S. Sailed for Earthquake relief duties at Sicilly
	31. 3.69	Sailed from Malta for Reserve at Gibraltar
	5.69	Renamed 'WARSASH' for Solent Division R.N.R.
	1. 1.76	Channel Group R.N.R.
	6. 6.77	Escort to H.M. Yacht 'BRITANNIA'
	28. 6.77	10th M.C.M.S. Fleet Review at Spithead
	23. 6.82	10th MC.M.S. North East Group R.N.R.

HMS Crofton

Name	Dates	Notes
CUXTON	13.10.54	Placed in Reserve
	8. 8.75	Completed refit at Gibraltar for 1st M.C.M.S.
	10.75	Commissioned — after 21 years in Reserve
	28. 6.77	Fishery Protection Squadron. Fleet Review
	25. 2.82	10th M.C.M.S. Tay Division R.N.R.
	6.10.82	Refitting at Gibraltar
	82-84	Tay Division R.N.R.

HMS Cuxton on the Synchrolift · HM Dockyard Rosyth

Name	Dates	Notes
DALSWINTON	1955-56	104th M.S.S.
	8.56-58	51st M.S.S. (Senior officer)
	1959	Operational Reserve Portsmouth
	1960-72	Tay Division R.N.R. as H.M.S. 'MONTROSE'
	3.72	For disposal
	4.73	Sold to Pounds, Portsmouth for B.U.
DARLASTON	1955-57	104th M.S.S. Took part in operation 'Musketeer'
	3. 3.60	With H.M.S. 'TYNE' at Agadir for earthquake relief duties (Operation 'Samaritan')
	24. 5.60	Sailed from Devonport for Singapore on transfer to Malaya, renamed 'MAHAMIRU'

Name	Dates	Notes
DARTINGTON	4.9.59	Commissioned at H.M.S. 'DILIGENCE' for 108th M.S.S.
	21.10.59	Sailed from Malta for Singapore
	30.11.59	Arrived Singapore 6th M.S.S.
	1960	Mine clearance operations Petan Bay
	17. 3.70	Sold to Wing Luen Hing, Hardwares Ltd. Hong Kong for B.U.
DERRITON	1955-66	H.M.S. 'KILLIECRANKIE'' Forth Division R.N.R.
	1967	Laid up at Hythe. Equipment stripped for use aboard 'WILTON'
	1969	For disposal
	23. 2.71	Sold to A.E. Pierce & Sons, Canvey Island, Essex B.U. at Kitson, Essex
DILSTON	1955-56	108th M.S.S.
	11/57	To Reserve at Hythe
	59-63	Operational Reserve Gibraltar
	1964	Sold to Malaya and renamed 'JERAI'
DUFTON	1955/1957	108th M.S.S.
	1958	104th M.S.S.
	1959	Reserve at Malta
	1960/1962	Operational Reserve Singapore
	23.4.62	Commissioned for 120th M.S.S.
	1967	Sailed from Far East with PENSTON & LANTON
	1967/69	10th M.C.M.S. London Division RNR as HMS THAMES.
	1969	For disposal
	10.6.77	Towed to Pounds Yard Portsmouth for BU.

HMS Dufton at Malta

Name	Dates	Notes
DUNKERTON	1955	Sold to South Africa, renamed 'PRETORIA'
DUMBLETON	27.10.58	Sold to South Africa at Hythe renamed 'PORT ELIZABETH'
	11.58	Sailed for South Africa
DURWESTON	1956	Sold to India as 'KAKINADA' (149th M.S.S.)
	11.56	Sailed for India (All ships sold to India were renamed after minor ports in India)
		Later 18th MCM 1980-81 Decommissioned
EDDERTON	1955-56	105th M.S.S.
	11.56	Operation Musketeer
	57/58	Reserve at Chatham
	58/64	Operational Reserve Hythe
	20. 7.64	Commissioned at Chatham as a Survey Ship and renamed 'MYRMIDON'
	1968	Sold to Malaya and renamed 'PERANTAU'

HMS Edderton after refit as HMS Myrmidon

Name	Dates	Notes
ESSINGTON	1955-56	108th M.S.S.
	1957-58	104th M.S.S. (Senior officer)
	1958	Sheerness refit
	1959-63	Operational Reserve Gibraltar
	1964	Sold to Malaya and renamed 'KINABALU'

Name	Dates	Notes
FENTON	1955-57	108th M.S.S.
	1958	Reducing to Reserve at Malta
	1959-63	Operational Reserve Aden
	3.67	For Disposal
	2. 7.68	Sold to Metal Recoveries (Newhaven) Ltd, for B.U.

HMS Fenton off Malta

Name	Dates	Notes
FISKERTON	15. 6.58	Commissioned at H.M.S. 'DILIGENCE' for 104th M.S.S.
	21.10.59	Sailed from Malta for Singapore
	30.11.59	Arrived Singapore for 6th M.S.S.
	1960	Petan Bay mine clearance operations
	3.70	Disposal List
	4.77	B.U. by Henderson-Morez Ltd, Dartford
FITTLETON	1956	Operational reserve at Hythe
	1960-9.76	H.M.S. 'CURZON' Sussex Division R.N.R.
	1. 1.76	Renamed 'FITTLETON' attached to Channel Group R.N.R. 10th M.C.M.S.
	20. 9.76	In collision with frigate H.M.S. 'MERMAID' when the two ships were engaged in ship to ship transfer off the Dutch coast. 'FITTLETON' capsized but remained afloat upside down for several hours before sinking in 160' of water. 12 members of her crew were lost.
	21. 9.76	Lifting operations carried out by floating crane 'MAGNUS' and taken to Den Helder
	4.10.76	Arrived Den Helder and beached
	9.10.76	Floated and taken in tow by tug 'ROYSTERER'
	11.10.76	Arrived Chatham Dockyard
	20. 9.77	Sold to Liguria Maritime Ltd, Sittingbourne

94

Name	Dates	Notes
FLOCKTON	1956	Operational Reserve at Hythe
	5.62	Taken out of Reserve at Hythe for 9th M.S.S. Persian Gulf
	3.69	For disposal
	5. 8.69	Sold for B.U. by Messrs Shipbreaking (Queensborough) Ltd, Kent
FLORISTON	1955/57	108th M.S.S.
	1958	Operational Reserve Malta
	3.11.59	Left Malta for Gib Reserve (under tow)
	59-67	Reserve Gib and UK
	27. 5.68	Sold for conversion to floating crane Messrs Pounds Shipowners and Shipbreakers, Havant, Hants
GAVINTON	1954/55	Operational Reserve Hythe
	1956-59	Vernon Squadron
	10.10.57	Trials—towed at 5 knots by Westland Whirl-wind Helicopter of the Special Trials Flight (705 Squadron) R.N.A.S. Lee-on-Solent. This was the first time a R.N. ship had been towed by Helicopter
	1960-62	S.O. Vernon Squadron
	1963-66	Operational Reserve
	1966/67	Conversion to Minehunter
	1968/71	9th M.S.S.
	1.72	1st M.C.M.S. Rosyth
	9.76-11.76	STANAVFORCHAN
	28. 6.77	Fleet review at Spithead
	10.80	Became the first vessel to be syncrolifted out of the water and wheeled into Rosyth Dock-yards new small ship refitting complex
	7.82-12.82	Attached to STANAVFORCHAN
	1983	1st M.S.S.
	1.1.84	3rd M.S.S.

HMS Gavinton

Name	Dates	Notes
GLASSERTON	1955	50th M.S.S.
	1962-66	3rd M.S.S.
	1966-79	3rd M.C.M.S.
	1. 5.70	Assisted in search for Canberra A/C which crashed in Lyme Bay
	1973	Patrol duties Northern Ireland during which time she inspected some 50 ships
	26. 9.75	Re-dedicated at H.M.S. 'DRAKE' on completion of refit
	28. 7.77	3rd M.C.M.S. Patrol duties at Fleet Review
	79-80	London Division R.N.R.
	3.81	Disposal List
	1983	Static RNR training ship on the Thames

HMS Glasserton (M1141) unarmed.

Name	Dates	Notes
HAZELTON	1955	Sold to South Africa renamed 'KAAPSTAD'
HEXTON	Nov 56	108th M.S.S.
	58-63	Operational Reserve Hythe/Chatham
	1963	Refitted for Malaysian Navy at Chatham
	10.63	Commissioned and renamed 'LEDANG'
HICKLETON	1955/58	108th M.S.S.
	2.2.59	To Malta Reserve
	1960-64	Reserve Singapore
	1965-66	On loan to Royal New Zealand Navy (11th M.S.S.) in Far East during Indonesian confrontation
	5.12.66	Arrived Portsmouth reverted to R.N.
	1967	Laid up at Hythe
	1967	Purchased by Argentina, refitted and modernised by Vospers, fitted with activated fin stabilisers in 1968 and renamed 'NEUQUEN' (M.1)

Name	Dates	Notes
HIGHBURTON		The first of the 'ton' class to be powered by Napier Deltic light-weight diesel machinery
	1955/56	105th M.S.S.
	1957	Operational Reserve Chatham - special trials
	1958-62	50th M.S.S. thence 3rd M.S.S.
	7.63	3rd M.C.M.S.-Operation 'Cableway'
	2.72	Reserve at Gibraltar
	10.72-3.75	Fishery Protection Squadron

HMS Highburton

Name	Dates	Notes
HODGESTON	1954-60	Renamed H.M.S. 'NORTHUMBRIA', Tyne Division R.N.R.
	1961-76	Renamed H.M.S. 'VENTURER', Severn Division R.N.R.
	1. 1.76	Renamed 'HODGESTON' South West Group R.N.R. 10th M.C.M.S.
	28. 6.77	Fleet Review, Spithead
	23. 6.82	10th M.C.M.S. North West Gruop R.N.R.
	1983	Clyde division R.N.R.
HOUGHTON	8.58	108th M.S.S. (S.O.)
	1959	104th M.S.S. (S.O.)
	21.10.59	Sailed from Malta for Singapore
	30.11.59	Arrived Singapore for 104th M.S.S.
	15.12.70	Arrived Devonport from Far East with WILKIESTON
	29. 1.71	Sold to Vickers & Son (Eng) Ltd., for commercial use at Plymouth and converted to tug

Name	Dates	Notes
HUBBERSTON	1956-63	Operational Reserve at Hythe
	4/63-64	Conversion to Minehunter at Chatham
	18.12.64	Commissioned at Chatham for 6th M.S.S.
	30. 6.65	Arrived Singapore
	1.10.71	Sailed from Hong Kong in company with 'BOSSINGTON' and 'MAXTON' for U.K. whilst on passage went to the assistance of H.M.S. 'ZULU'. Together with 'BOSSINGTON' took 'ZULU' in tow for Dakar
	3. 1.72	Senior Officer 2nd M.C.M.S. based at H.M.S. 'VERNON'
	1.11.74	Attached to STANAVFORCHAN
	—4.75	Operation 'Rheostat Two'
	4. 7.75	Returned to U.K.
	6.76-9.76	Attached to STANAVFORCHAN
	9.78-5.79	Attached to STANAVFORCHAN
	23. 7.82	2nd M.C.M.S. Portsmouth

HMS Hubberston - sails from Hong Kong.

ILMINGTON	1955-56	105th M.S.S.
	1957-66	Operational Reserve Hythe
	1967	Sold to Argentina
	18. 4.68	At Portsmouth for refit
	19. 7.68	Commissioned at Portsmouth as a minehunter and renamed 'FORMOSA' (M.6)

Name	Dates	Notes
INVERMORISTON	1955	104th M.S.S. (Harwich)
	1956	At Chatham—Operational Reserve
	1957-64	Operational Reserve, Hythe
	2.65—	11th M.S.S. Far East during confrontation
	10.66	with Indonesia
	5.11.66	Arrived Portsmouth from Far East with 'SANTON'
	7.67	After refitting at Portsmouth was manned by P.A.S. based at Milford as a night safety ship for aircraft operating from R.N.A.S. Brawdy
	3.68	With 'CLARBESTON' and 'SHOULTON' (see 'CLARBESTON' 6 bodies recovered
	7.71	B.U. at Newport

HMS Invermoriston at Singapore

IVESTON	1956-62	Operational Reserve at Hythe
	3.1.63	Towed to Devonport
	1/63-7/64	Conversion to Minehunter at Devonport
	16.10.64	1st M.C.M.S.
	8.68	Operation 'New Broom'
	1.72	2nd M.C.M.S. Portsmouth
	29. 7.75	Rescued Pilot of twin-engined A/C which ditched 5 miles off Isle of Wight
	11.76-12.76	STANAVFORCHAN
	28. 6.77	2nd M.C.M.S. Fleet Review Spithead

99

Name	Dates	Notes
JACKTON	1956	Operational Reserve at Hythe
	1961	Refitted in U.K. for Australian Navy. Re-engined with Deltic engines
	30. 8.62	Commissioned and renamed H.M.A.S. 'TEAL'
	1.10.62	Sailed from Portsmouth for Australia

HMAS Teal (ex Jackton)

Name	Dates	Notes
KEDLESTON	1955-62	Operational Reserve Hythe
	2.7.62	Towed to Gibraltar (Reserve)
	10. 7.66	Arrived Plymouth in tow of tug 'CYCLONE' for conversion to Minehunter
	23.1.69	Commissioned at Devonport for Fishery Protection Squadron
	1. 1.76	10th M.C.M.S. North East Group R.N.R.
	28. 6.77	Fleet Review at Spithead—10th M.C.M.S. Forth Division R.N.R.
KELLINGTON	1956	Operational Reserve at Hythe
	1967	Conversion to Minehunter at Chatham
	6. 6.69	Commissioned at Chatham for F.P.S.
	1.1.77	Transferred from FPS to Sussex Division R.N.R.
	28. 6.77	Fleet Review Spithead. 10th M.C.M.S.
	Dec 81/82	Long refit at Rosyth.
KEMERTON	1956	Operational Reserve at Hythe
	1962	Taken out of Reserve at Hythe for 9th M.S.S. Persian Gulf
	1965	9th M.S.S. Persian Gulf
	15.11.66	Arrived Portsmouth from Far East for disposal
	5.69	
	1975	B.U. at Poole

Name	Dates	Notes
KILDARTON	1956	108th M.S.S. Mediterranean
	1956-60	104th M.S.S.
	1966-67	9th M.S.S. Persian Gulf
	1967	Laid up at Hythe
	9.69	Portsmouth for disposal and Conversion to oil rig supply ship
	1971	Sold as a Survey ship to South Ocean Services Southampton

M/V Kildarton

KIRKLISTON	14. 8.56	'KILMOREY', Ulster Division R.N.R.
	1964	1st of the 'ton' class to conversion as a Mine-hunter. Conversion carried out at Portsmouth
	1. 4.69	Arrived Hong Kong 6th M.S.S.
	22. 5.72	With 'SHERATON' sailed from Hong Kong
	8.72	Arrived H.M.S. 'LOCHINVAR'—1st M.C.M.S.
	1973	Refitted at Gibraltar
	1974	Manned by R.N.R. for exercise Northern Merger (first time a minehunter manned by R.N.R.)
	8.75-12.75	STANAVFORCHAN
	8.77- 1.78	
	1.82- 7.82	
	9.82	2nd M.C.M.S. with 'NURTON' carried out Sonar Searches in English Channel between Folkestone and Sangate in preparation for four new electricity power cables to be laid across the Channel

Name	Dates	Notes
LALESTON	7.56	Vernon Squadron
	1964	In Reserve
	22. 3.67	Re-commissioned after conversion to Diving Trials Ship when all sweep gear was removed and replaced by a Diving Store, decompression chamber and other equipment
	28. 6.77	Fleet Review at Spithead
		Ulster Division R.N.R.
	8.82	Laid up at Rosyth for disposal

HMS Laleston

Name	Dates	Notes
LANTON	1956—	Operational Reserve at Hythe
	1962-67	8th M.S.S.
	3.68	For disposal
	24. 4.70	Sold to C.H. Rugg & Co. Ltd, for B.U.
LETTERSTON	11.56	104th M.S.S. (Operation Musketeer)
	1.65	Joined F.P.S. replaced 'WATCHFUL'
	8.69	Arrived Portsmouth to pay off for disposal
	9. 6.71	Sold to C.H. Rugg & Co. Ltd, on behalf of Jacques Bakkar & Zonen, Bruges, Belgium for B.U.
LEVERTON	1955-57	108th M.S.S.
	1963	7th M.S.S. (Malta)
	31. 3.69	Sailed from Malta for Reserve at Gibraltar
	3.71	For disposal
	1971	Commercial Salvage vessel
	4.72	Sold to Pounds, Portsmouth for B.U.

Name	Dates	Notes
LEWISTON	16.6.60	The last of the 'ton' class to be built, joined 100th M.S.S.
	1963	2nd M.S.S.
	5.63	Senior Officer 2nd M.S.S. Operation 'Clear Road'.
	7.63	Operation 'Cable Way'
	9.9.63	Operation 'Ice Scot'
	6.65	Transferred from 2nd M.S.S. to Vernon Squadron
	5.1.66	Sailed from Portsmouth for Port Edgar and 1st M.C.M.S.
	7.69	Western Fleet Review at Torbay
	3.72	2nd M.C.M.S.
	1981-82	10th M.C.M.S. London Division R.N.R.

HMS Lullington

LULLINGTON	8.12.56	Commissioned at H.M.S. 'DILLIGENCE' Hythe for 104th M.S.S.
	12.1.57	Sailed from Hythe to Malta
	1957-58	104th M.S.S. Mediterranean. Malta/Cyprus
	8.58	Aden
	1959	Reserve at Singapore
	18.1.60	Commissioned at Singapore for 11th M.S.S.
	1.65	Reserve at Singapore crew transferred to H.M.S. 'KILDARTON'
	2.65	Recommissioned 11th M.S.S.
	4.66	Refitted at Singapore for Malaysian Navy
	5.66	Renamed 'TAHAN'

Name	Dates	Notes
MADDISTON	1956-7	108th M.S.S.
	19.58-61	Operational Reserve Aden.
	1962	Gibraltar Refit - thence Malta Reserve
	28.8.69	Arrived Hythe in tow of tug 'BUSTLER'
	4.2.75	Arrived Kitson Vickers Ltd., Sunderland for B.U.
MAXTON	1958-59	104th M.S.S.
	24.12.58	In collision with H.M.S. 'UNDAUNTED' off Larnaca
	1959-62	108th M.S.S.
	1962-65	Operational Reserve Hythe
	1966	Conversion to Minehunter at Devonport
	1967-71	6th M.S.S.
	1.10.71	Sailed from Far East to UK
	1972-73	2nd M.C.M.S.
	4.74-11.74	Operation 'Rheostat' (Egypt)
	28.6.71	Fleet Review Spithead.
	1974-83	1st M.C.M.S. (Rosyth)

HMS Maryton

Name	Dates	Notes
MARYTON	20.1.59	Commissioned at H.M.S. 'DILIGENCE' 104th M.S.S.
	6.11.59	Sailed from Malta for Singapore
	12.59	Arrived Singapore
	8.64	Shelled by Indonesian Shore battery, shells fell short
	8.64	Sailed from Singapore for patrol of Tawau, prior to reaching Labuab Island she struck a large floating log, damaging port propeller, returned Singapore for new screw and 300 square feet of sheathing.
	25.3.65	Fired on by Indonesian vessel off Johore by Mortars, Machine gun and rifles. 3 of crew slightly injured
	12.10.67	Sailed from Far East for UK
	18.12.67	Arrived Portsmouth
	1969	Conversion to Oil rig supply ship
	5.7.69	Sold to Messrs. Shipbreaking (Queensborough) Ltd., Kent for B.U.

Name	Dates	Notes
MONKTON	1957-59	In Reserve
	1959-65	Vernon Squadron
	1.66	1st M.C.M.S. Port Edgar
	8.68	Operation 'New Broom'
	1971	Conversion to Patrol Craft
	9.1.72	Sailed from Devonport
	28.4.72	Arrived Hong Kong 6th Patrol Craft Squadron. (P.1055)

HMS Monkton

Name	Dates	Notes
NURTON	1958	Renamed H.M.S. 'MONTROSE' Tay Division R.N.R.
	1960-63	5th M.S.S.
	5.63	Operation 'Clear Road'
	1965	Conversion to Minehunter at Portsmouth
	1966	1st M.C.M.S. Port Edgar
	8.68	Operation 'New Broom'
	9.72	2nd M.C.M.S.
	1972	Renamed 'KILLIECRANKIE' Forth Division R.N.R. 10th M.C.M.S.
	11.74--	
	12.74	STANAVFORCHAN
	1.1.75-	
	29.8.75	STANAVFORCHAN
	28.6.77	2nd M.C.M.S. Fleet Review Spithead
	1.81-7.81	STANAVFORCHAN
	9.82	With 'KIRKLISTON' carried out Sonar Search of English Channel (See 'KIRKLISTON')
	24.2.83	In collision with 'BROCKLESBY' off Portland
	9.3.83	Arrived Portsmouth in tow of tug CONFIANCE, for repairs

Name	Dates	Notes
OAKINGTON	1959	Sold to South Africa renamed 'MOSSELBAAI'
OULSTON	1956	No RN Service. Reserve at Hythe
	8.12.70	Sold to Ireland renamed 'GRAINNE' (CM10)
	30.1.71	Commissioned at Portsmouth

Grainne (Ex. Oulston)

Name	Dates	Notes
OVERTON	8.56	Transferred to India renamed 'KARWAR'
	11.56	Sailed for India as leader of 149th M.S.S.
	1980-81	Decommissioned.
PACKINGTON	1959	Sold to South Africa — renamed 'WALVISBAAI'

Name	Dates	Notes
PENSTON	24.8.56	Commissioned at Hythe for 108th M.S.S.
	1956-57	108th M.S.S. Mediterranean
	1958	Operational Reserve Malta
	1959-61	Operational Reserve Aden
	11/61	Towed to Singapore
	23.4.62	Commissioned at Singapore (with DUFTON & LANTON to replace Ham Class) for 120th M.S.S. (thence 8th M.S.S.)
	1967	Sailed for UK and Hythe Reserve
	3.69	For disposal
	6.2.70	Sold to Metal Recoveries Newhaven Ltd.

HMS Penston sails from Singapore Feb 1967 for UK (with Dufton & Lanton)

Name	Dates	Notes
PICTON	1956	Reserve at Hythe
	57/62	Operational reserve at Hythe
	63	Chatham refit thence Singapore reserve
	1.65	Commissioned at Singapore 11th M.S.S.
	5.12.66	Arrived Portsmouth from Far East
	8.69	For disposal
	5.9.69	Sold to Messrs. Shipbreaking (Queensborough) Ltd., Kent for B.U.
POLLINGTON	17.10.59	Machinery Conversion & accepted by Mersey Division R.N.R.
	1.76	Reverted to Pollington
	Feb 78	FPS
	1979-83	Fishery Protection Squadron

Name	Dates	Notes
PUNCHESTON	1959	104th M.S.S. Mediterranean
	21.10.59	Sailed from Malta for Singapore
	30.11.59	Arrived Singapore 6th M.S.S.
	17.4.66	Fired on by Indonesian Shore battery — 100 round fell approx. 800 yards short
	1967	9th M.S.S. Persian Gulf
	1971	Returned to UK
	3.72	For disposal
	1972	Sold to Pounds, Portsmouth for B.U. by Henderson Merez Ltd.

HMS Puncheston (note Arabic pennant numbers)

Name	Dates	Notes
QUAINTON	1959	Reserve
	1960-72	'NORTHUMBRIA' Tyne Division R.N.R. 10th M.S.S.
	3.72	Laid up at Devonport for disposal
	11/79	BU Tyne

HMS Rennington

RENNINGTON	1958	To Reserve at Hythe on completion
	1960-63	Reserve at Gibraltar
	1966	For disposal
	1968	Sold to Argentina renamed 'CHACO' (M.5)
		Converted to Minehunter at Portsmouth
REPTON	1958-61	Operational Reserve at Hythe
	1962-63	5th M.S.S. Vernon Squadron
	5.63	Operation 'Clear Road'
	6.71	'CLYDE' Clyde Division R.N.R. 10th M.C.M.S.
	1.1.76	Renamed 'REPTON' North West Group R.N.R. 10th M.C.M.S.
	1979-80	F.P.S.
	3.80	For disposal
	8.82	Laid up at Rosyth
	11.82	Towed to Pounds, Portsmouth
RODINGTON	1955-57	108th M.S.S.
	1957	Rosyth Refit for reserve
	1958	Operational Reserve Rosyth
	1959z560	Operational Reserve Gibraltar
	1960-62	108th M.S.S.
	7.62	Reserve at Gibraltar
	1972	B.U. at Fleetwood

Name	Dates	Notes
SANTON	14.8.56	Navigational Training Portsmouth. Commissioned as Tender to H.M.S. Redpole while Redpole — non operational.
	1957-58	108th M.S.S.
	1958-59	Operational Reserve Malta
	1960-64	Operational Reserve Singapore
	10.4.64	Commissioned at Singapore manned by Royal New Zealand Navy for 11th M.S.S. Borneo/Indonesian confrontation.
	5.11.66	Arrived Portsmouth from Far East with 'INVERMORISTON'
	1967	Laid up at Hythe and purchased by Argentina
	1968	Refitted at Vosper Thornycroft, modernised and fitted with activator fin stabiliser equipment. Renamed 'CHABUT' (M.7)
SEFTON	1955-57	108th M.S.S. (SO)
	1958	Operational Reserve Malta
	1959-63	Operational Reserve Aden
	2.7.68	Sold to C.H. Rugg & Co. Ltd. London on behalf of Jacques Bakkar & Zonnen, Bruges, Belgium for B.U.

HMS Shavington

Name	Dates	Notes
SHAVINGTON	1956-69	108th M.S.S. Mediterranean (later 7th M.S.S.)
	31.3.69	7th M.S.S. Sailed from Malta for Reserve at Gibraltar
	25.4.69	At Gibraltar — Reserve
	9.74	F.P.S.
	28.6.77	Fleet Review Spithead F.P.S.
	23.6.82	10th M.C.M.S. North West Group R.N.R.
	1983/4	Ulster Division R.N.R.

HM Ships Sefton & Santon (top) in the Mediterranean

Name	Dates	Notes
SHERATON	1959	Vernon Squadron
	7.63	Operation 'Cableway' 5th M.S.S.
	4.5.65	Conversion to Minehunter at Portsmouth
	25.8.65	Sailed for Far East 6th M.S.S.
	22.5.72	Sailed from Hong Kong with 'KIRKLISTON' for UK
	8.72	Arrived H.M.S. 'LOCHNIVAR' joined 1st M.S.S.
	4.75	Suez Canal Clearance
	80-82	Refitting.
	82/83	1st M.C.M.S.
	1.1.84	SO of M.C.M. 3 (Reformed)

HMS Shoulton — no armament or Loop. Note pump jet over stern

Name	Dates	Notes
SHOULTON	1957	Conversion to prototype minehunter at Vosper Thornycroft, Woolston, prototype minehunter.
	1958	At Portland (attached to 2nd T.S.)
	26.8.60	Sailed from Portland for U.S.A.
	11.60	50th M.S.S.
	7.63	Senior Officer 1st M.S.S. Operation 'Cableway'
	16.4.64	Sailed from Port Edgar with 'YARNTON' for operation 'Clear Road'
	1965-67	Refitted with pump jet propulsion
	3.68	With 'CLARBESTON' and 'INVERMORISTON' (See 'CLARBESTON')
	1.5.70	Assisted in search for Canberra aircraft which crashed in Lyme Bay with 'GLASSERTON'
	28.7.77	Senior Officer 3rd M.C.M.S. Patrol Duties at Fleet Review, Spithead.
	12.79	Paid off
	17.4.81	Arrived Blyth for B.U.

Name	Dates	Notes
SINGLETON	1961/62	Refitted in UK for Australian Navy. Converted to 'Deltic' main engines. Enclosed bridge, air conditioning and stabilisers fitted.
	11.9.62	Commissioned as H.M.A.S. 'IBIS'
	1.10.62	Sailed from Portsmouth for Australia.
SOBERTON	1958-63	F.P.S.
	5.63	Operation 'Clear Road'
	28/29.7.69	Western Fleet Review at Torbay
	14.12.79	Recommissioned at Chatham for F.P.S. on completion of refit.

HMS Soberton

Name	Dates	Notes
SOMERLEYTON	1956-60	Operational Reserve at Hythe
	1961/62	Refitted in UK for Australian Navy as 'SINGLETON' (QV)
	18.7.62	Commissioned at Portsmouth as H.M.A.S. 'HAWKE'
	1.10.62	Sailed from Portsmouth for Australia
STRATTON	7.1.59	Completed
	1959	Sold to South Africa renamed 'KIMBERLEY'

Name	Dates	Notes
STUBBINGTON	12.57/61	108th M.S.S. Mediterranean
	1961/2	Aden
	1962-69	7th M.S.S. Mediterranean
	15.1.68	Sailed from Malta for Sicily - earthquake relief.
	5.69	Navigation Tender at Portsmouth
	6.72-1976	H.M.S. 'MONTROSE' Tay Division R.N.R. 10th M.C.M.S.
	18.6.77	Commissioned at Chatham on completion of 14 month refit for duty in F.P.S.

HMS Stubbington

Name	Dates	Notes
SULLINGTON	1955-56	50th M.S.S.
	1956-57	Portland. Tender to H.M.S. 'OSPREY'
	1958-63	Operational Reserve Hythe
	17.7.64	Converted to Coastal Survey Ship at Devonport renamed 'MERMAID'
	9.70	Sold to H.K. Vickers & Son (Eng) Ltd., Sheffield for B.U. at Plymouth — towed to Fleetwood for final dismantling
SWANSTON	1956/9	In reserve
	19.7.62	Commissioned and renamed H.M.A.S. 'GULL'
	1.10.62	Sailed from Portsmouth for Australia
TARLTON	1956	Reserve/Docking & Repairs — Chatham
	1966	For disposal
	1967	Purchased by Argentina
	1968	Refitted and modernised by Vosper Thornycroft, renamed 'RIO NEGRO' (M.2)

Name	Dates	Notes
THANKERTON	1957/59	108th M.S.S.
	1959-60	Operational Reserve Malta
	1960-64	Operational Reserve Singapore
	1965-66	11th M.S.S. Far East
	4.66	Refitted at Singapore and transferred to Malayia — renamed 'BRINCHANG'

HMS Upton — the last RN Operational Minesweeper. All the remainder being FPS or RNR

UPTON	Aug-Dec 56	Operation Musketeer (105th M.S.S.)
	1957-65	100th M.S.S. (Later 2nd M.S.S.)
	5.63	Operation 'Clear Road'
	5.1.66	Sailed from Portsmouth to join 1st M.C.M.S. at Port Edgar
	8.68	Operation 'New Broom'
	7.69	Western Fleet Review Torbay
	1970/2	2nd M.C.M.S. as Training Minesweeper
	9.73	1st M.C.M.S. at Rosyth
	1975	Renamed 'NORTHUMBRIA', Tyne Division R.N.R. 10th M.C.M.S.
	1.1.76	Renamed 'UPTON' North East Group R.N.R. 10th M.C.M.S.
	5.4.76	Sailed for Gibraltar extended refit
	28.6.77	Fleet Review, Spithead. 10th M.C.M.S.
	1980-83	1st M.C.M.S. as Training Vessel vice Lewiston
	1.4.84	F.P.S.

Name	Dates	Notes
WALKERTON	1958	104th M.S.S. Mediterranean
	8.58	Aden
	63-69	Senior Officer - 7th M.S.S. Mediterranean
	31.3.69	7th M.S.S. Sailed from Malta for reserve at Gibraltar
	1.70	Conversion refit for Dartmouth Training duties.
	1971	Tender to B.R.N.C. Dartmouth
	1980/83	F.P.S.

HMS Walkerton — armament removed & chartroom fitted in lieu of loop during service as BRNC tender.

Name	Dates	Notes
WASPERTON	4/58-68	F.P.S.
	1971	Refitted as a Patrol Craft at Rosyth (P.1089)
	9.1.72	Sailed from Plymouth for Far East
	28.4.72	Arrived Hong Kong and joined 6th Patrol Craft Squadron
WENNINGTON	8.56	Sold to India renamed 'CUDDALORE' 149th M.S.S.
	1980-81	Decommissioned
WHITTON	8.56	Sold to India renamed 'CANNAMORE' 149th M.S.S.
	1980-81	Decommissioned

HMS Wilkieston

Name	Dates	Notes
WILKIESTON	1958	104th M.S.S. Mediterranean
	8.58	Aden
	21.10.59	Sailed from Malta for Singapore
	30.11.59	Arrived Singapore 6th M.S.S.
	1969	6th M.S.S.
	15.12.70	Arrived Portsmouth from Far East via Pacific
	1972	Sales List
	8.76	B.U. at St. Davids
WILTON	11.2.70	Contract signed for the construction
	18.1.72	Launched Bows first from her covered and heated building berth. Equipment from the scrapped 'DERRITON' was installed after overhaul, but new engines were provided.
	25.4.73	Joined 2nd M.C.M.S. at Portsmouth
	7.4.74	Operation Rheostat (Suez Canal)
	21.11.74	2nd M.C.M.S. Portsmouth
	1.77-6.77	STANAVFORCHAN
	28.6.77	Senior Officer 2nd M.C.M.S. Spithead Fleet Review
	5.79-1.80	STANAVFORCHAN
	23.6.82	2nd M.C.M.S.

Name	Dates	Notes
WISTON	6/60	To 100th M.S.S. vice APPLETON
	1963	2nd M.S.S.
	5.63	Operation 'Clear Road'
	9.9.63	Operation Ice Scot
	6.65	2nd M.S.S. transferred to Vernon Squadron
	5.1.66	Sailed from Portsmouth for Port Edgar to join 1st M.S.S.
	1968	9th M.S.S. Senior Officer, Persian Gulf
	1971	Sailed from Bahrein for UK — leaks in hull, necessitated repairs at Gibraltar
	1972-76	'NORTHUMBRIA', Tyne Division R.N.R. 10th M.C.M.S.
	28.6.77	Fleet Review, Spithead 10th M.C.M.S. R.N.R.
	1977	For disposal
	8.82	Laid up at Rosyth

HMS Wiston

Name	Dates	Notes
WOLVERTON	1957	100th M.S.S.
	1963	2nd M.S.S.
	8.68	Operation 'New Broom'
	1970	1st M.C.M.S.
	1971	Refitted at Rosyth as Patrol Craft
	9.1.72	Sailed from Plymouth for Hong Kong
	28.4.72	Arrived Hong Kong 6th Patrol Craft Squadron (P.1093)
	29.9.80	Captured 230 illegal immigrants in Hong Kong waters

HMS Woolaston—a rare photograph—camouflaged at the time of Indonesian Confrontation.

Name	Dates	Notes
WOOLASTON	1958	104th M.S.S.
	11.58	Operational Reserve Hythe
	10.59	Sailed from Malta for Singapore
	1960-62	104th M.S.S.
	1963-68	6th M.S.S.
	29.4.69	Renamed 'THAMES' London Division R.N.R.
	1975	Renamed 'WOOLASTON'
	3.76	For disposal
	1/81	Towed from Portsmouth for scrap
WOTTON	4.58-67	F.P.S.
	8.68	Operation 'New Broom'
	Aug 71	Replaced by 'BRINTON' in F.P.S.
	1.72	3rd M.C.M.S. Portland
	17.10.75	Arrived Penzance to take part in a ceremony to commemorate the arrival there of H.M.S. 'PICKLE' in 1805 with the news of Nelson's death and Victory at Trafalgar.
	5/78	F.P.S. after long refit
	1.4.83	Relieved in F.P.S. by UPTON thence to R.N.R. Tyne
YARNTON	15.5.57	100th M.S.S.
	1963	2nd M.S.S.
	5.63	Operation 'Clear Road'
	9.9.63	Operation 'Ice Scot'
	16.4.64	Operation 'Clear Road Two'
	1965	9th M.S.S. Persian Gulf
	1971	Refitted as Patrol Craft at Taikoo Shipyard Hong Kong for 6th Patrol Craft Squadron (P.1096)

HMS Yarnton in the Persian Gulf

H.M.S. WILTON (M.1116).

Displacement:	450 tons (Full load).
Dimensions:	145(wl) 153(oa) x 28.8 x 8.5′
Armament:	1-40mm Mark 7.
Machinery:	2 English Electric Deltic 18-7A diesels; 2 shafts; 3000 bhp = 16 knots.
Range, Miles:	2,300 at 13 knots.
Complement:	37 (5 officers & 32 ratings).

Built to the existing minehunter design. Similar in appearance to the "Conventional" ton class. Fitted with reconditioned machinery and equipment from the scrapped DERRITON. Twin active rudders (fitted with small propellers). Four 60 Kw generators.

Notes — See Page 117

H.M.Ships ST DAVID & VENTURER

Builders:	Cubow Ltd., Woolwich
Displacement:	392 tons gross
Dimensions:	120.7′ x 29.2′ x 12.8′
Main Engines:	2 Mirrlees-Blackstone Diesels, 2000 hp = 14 knots
Armament	None
Complement:	35

Two commercial trawlers were chartered by the MOD (N) on 1st November, 1978 formerly the SUFFOLK MONARCH and SUFFOLK HARVESTER, owned by Small & Co., (Lowestoft) Ltd. Both were originally designed as Stern Trawlers and the most advanced to join Small and Co's modern fleet at Lowestoft.

The two trawlers were renamed ST. DAVID (MO.7) (SUFFOLK MONARCH) and VENTURER (MO.8) and converted to minesweepers at Lowestoft by a subsidiary of Small & Co.

ST. DAVID arrived at Portsmouth on 30th November, 1978 whilst VENTURER was commissioned at Bristol during December, 1978.

Both ships have been allocated to the R.N.R. (10th MCMS) ST DAVID to the South Wales Division at Cardiff. VENTURER to the Severn Division at Bristol. They were equipped for deep team sweeping and operated together as a pair.

Both ships returned to their civilian owners in Nov 83 on completion of their charters.

INSHORE MINESWEEPERS — HAM CLASS

Displacement:	120 tons (standard) 159 (full load)
Dimensions:	100 (pp) 106 5/12 (0a) x 21 1/6 x 5½ '
Guns:	1 - 40mm Bofors A.A. or 1 - 20mm Oerlikon A.A.
Machinery:	2 Paxman diesels BHP 550 = 14 knots (9 knots sweeping)
Oil Fuel:	15 tons
Complement:	15 (peacetime) 22 (war)

Name	PT No	Completed	Builders
ABBOTSHAM	M.2787	10. 1.57	Blackmore
ALTHAM	M.2602	8. 7.53	Camper Nicholson
ARLINGHAM	M.2603	24.11.53	Camper Nicholson
ASHELDHAM	M.2604	9. 9.53	Philip & Son
BASSINGHAM	M.2605	1.10.53	Vospers
BEDHAM	M.2606	18.12.53	Bolson
BIRDHAM	M.2785	5. 3.57	J. Taylor
BISHAM	M.2607	2. 7.54	Bolson
BLUNHAM	M.2608	11. 6.53	Brooke Marine
BODENHAM	M.2609	23. 9.53	Brooke Marine
BOREHAM	M.2610	16.12.53	Brooke Marine
BOTTISHAM	M.2611	21.10.53	Ailsa
BRANTINGHAM	M.2612	2. 7.54	Ailsa
BRIGHAM	M.2613	22.12.53	Berthon Boat
BUCKLESHAM	M.2614	30. 4.54	Ardrossan
CARDINGHAM	M.2615	17. 7.53	Herd & Mackenzie
CHELSHAM	M.2616	15. 7.53	Jones (Buckie)
CHILLINGHAM	M.2617	17. 6.53	McLean & Sons
COBHAM	M.2618	1. 7.53	Fairlie Yacht
CRANHAM	M.2701	1. 6.54	J. Samuel White
DAMERHAM	M.2629	19. 3.54	Brooke Marine
DARSHAM	M.2619	21.12.53	Jones (Buckie)
DAVENHAM	M.2620	8.12.53	Weatherhead
DITTISHAM	M.2621	29. 6.54	Fairlie Yacht
DOWNHAM	M.2622	27. 3.56	J. Samuel White
EDLINGHAM	M.2623	16. 9.55	Weatherhead
ELSENHAM	M.2624	11. 1.56	Ailsa
ETCHINGHAM	M.2625	27. 6.58	Ailsa
EVERINGHAM	M.2626	14. 7.54	Philip & Son
FELMERSHAM	M.2627	11. 5.54	Camper Nicholson
FLINTHAM	M.2628	1.11.55	Bolson
FORDHAM	M.2717	13.12.56	Jones (Buckie)
FRETTENHAM	M.2702	14. 9.54	J. Samuel White
FRITHAM	M.2630	7. 7.54	Brooke Marine
GEORGEHAM	M.2788	5.11.57	P.K. Harris
GLENTHAM	M.2631	20. 5.58	Ardrossan
GREETHAM	M.2632	5. 2.55	Herd & McKenzie
HALSHAM	M.2633	9. 7.54	Jones (Buckie)
HARPHAM	M.2634	22.12.54	Jones (Buckie)
HAVERSHAM	M.2635	22.10.54	McLean
HILDERSHAM	M.2705	9.11.54	Vosper
HOVERINGHAM	M.2637	11. 7.56	Fairlee Yacht
INGLESHAM	M.2601	13. 5.53	J. Samuel White
ISHAM	M.2703	25. 1.55	J. Samuel White

Name	PT No	Completed	Builders
KINGHAM	M.2704	1. 6.55	J. Samuel White
LASHAM	M.2636	16. 9.54	Weatherhead
LEDSHAM	M.2706	22. 3.55	Bolson
LITTLESHAM	M.2707	19.11.54	Brooke Marine
LUDHAM	M.2708	30. 3.55	Fairlee Yacht
MALHAM	M.2789	10.12.58	Fairlee Yacht
MERSHAM	M.2709	14. 1.55	P.K. Harris
MICKLEHAM	M.2710	10. 5.55	Berthon Boat
MILEHAM	M.2711	16. 3.55	Blackmore
NEASHAM	M.2712	15.11.57	J. Samuel White
NETTLEHAM	M.2713	21. 2.58	J. Samuel White
OCKHAM	M.2714	5.11.59	Ailsa
ODIHAM	M.2783	27. 7.56	Vospers
OTTRINGHAM	M.2715	17.12.58	McLean
PAGHAM	M.2716	22. 3.56	Jones (Buckie)
PETERSHAM	M.2718	9. 3.55	McLean
PINEHAM	M.2719	22. 7.55	McLean
POLSHAM	M.2792	6. 4.60	M. Giles
POPHAM	M.2782	4.10.55	Vospers
PORTISHAM	M.2781	26. 3.56	Dorset Yacht
POWDERHAM	M.2720	27. 5.60	J. Samuel White
PULHAM	M.2721	10. 1.56	Saunders Roe
PUTTENHAM	M.2784	9. 5.58	Thornycroft
RACKHAM	M.2722	26. 6.56	Saunders Roe
RAMPISHAM	M.2786	18.10.57	Bolson
REEDHAM	M.2723	20.11.58	Saunders Roe
RENDLESHAM	M.2724	25. 2.55	Brooke Marine
RIPLINGHAM	M.2725	1. 7.55	Brooke Marine
SANDRINGHAM	M.2791	11. 9.57	McLean
SAXLINGHAM	M.2727	29. 1.57	Berthon Boat
SHIPHAM	M.2726	3. 2.56	Brooke Marine
SHRIVENHAM	M.2728	11. 8.56	Bolson
SIDLESHAM	M.2729	23.11.55	P.K. Harris
SPARHAM	M.2731	26. 7.55	Vospers
STEDHAM	M.2730	28. 7.55	Blackmore
SULHAM	M.2732	21. 7.55	Fairlee Yacht
THAKEHAM	M.2733	15.11.57	Fairlee Yacht
THATCHAM	M.2790	17. 4.58	Jones (Buckie)
THORNHAM	M.2793	20. 6.58	J. Taylor
TIBENHAM	M.2734	28. 4.55	McGroer
TONGHAM	M.2735	18. 6.57	J. Miller
TRESHAM	M.2736	10.11.55	M. Giles
WARMINGHAM	M.2737	30.11.56	Thornycroft
WEXHAM	M.2738	11. 1.55	J. Taylor
WHIPPINGHAM	M.2739	21. 6.55	J. Taylor
WINTRINGHAM	M.2777	8.12.55	J. Samuel White
WOLDINGHAM	M.2778	17. 7.57	J. Samuel White
WRENTHAM	M.2779	6. 7.55	Dorset Yacht
YAXHAM	M.2780	19. 3.59	J. Samuel White

Name	Dates	Notes
ABBOTSHAM	11.57-65	Operational Reserve Rosneath
	1966	Disposal List.
	31.8.67	Pounds, Portsmouth.
	1969	Agricultural Vehicles Oxford Ltd.
ALTHAM	13.7.53	Commissioned at HMS Diligence, Hythe.
	1954/56	232nd M/S.
	1957	Reserve at Rosneath.
	1.4.59	Malayan Navy as SRI JOHOR.
ARLINGHAM	11.54-59	Operational Reserve Gosport
	1966-67	Conversion to TRV at Devonport, thence Guardship at Gibraltar.
	19.9.78	Sold.

HMS Arlington (as Gibraltar Guardship)

Name	Dates	Notes
ASHELDHAM	1954/56	232nd M/S.
	1957	Reserve.
	1958	Reserve at Chatham, preservation and preparation for shipment to Far East.
	1.4.59	Malayan Navy as SRI PERLIS.
BASSINGHAM	1954/56	232nd M/S.
	1958/60	On loan to East African Navy.
	9.10.61	Returned to R.N. Control.
	11.1.66	Pounds Yard, Portsmouth for Yacht conversion.
BEDHAM	1954-56	Reserve at Portsmouth
	1956	Refit at Shoreham
	12.8.58	Malayan Navy as SRI LANKA SUKA.

Name	Dates	Notes
BIRDHAM	1957-64	Operational Reserve Rosneath
	1964	Brought forward from Reserve for RNXS.
	5.80	Arrived Great Wakering, Essex for BU.

HMS Birdham before RNXS conversion

Name	Dates	Notes
BISHAM	1954-56	Operational Reserve Gosport
	29.9.56	Extensively damaged by fire.
	8.8.57	Pounds, Portsmouth for BU.
BLUNHAM	1954	232nd M.S.S. - Chatham
	1955-56	Operational Reserve Gosport
	1957-63	Operational Reserve Roseneath
	1967	South Yemen Navy.
BODENHAM	1954-55	Tender to HMS VERNON
	1956-63	Operational Reserve Rosneath
	1967	South Yemen Navy.
BOREHAM	5.3.56	Malayan Navy, renamed SRI JERONG.
	1954-60	Operational Reserve Gosport
	1960-65	Operational Reserve Singapore
BOTTISHAM	1954/5	Operational Reserve Hythe/Gosport
	1956/7	Poole refit thence Sheerness Reserve
	1958-65	Operational Reserve Hythe
	11.1.66	Transferred to R.A.F. after refitting at Hythe (HMFA 5000) replaced target towing vessel at Plymouth.
	1971	Returned to R.N. Control.
	23.11.73	Sold to Gomba Marina Ltd.
BRANTINGHAM	1955/56	Operational Reserve Gosport
	2.11.57	Left Aden with BEDHAM as deck cargo in SS BENARTY for Singapore
	1.11.58	Malayan Navy as SRI TEMASEK.
BRIGHAM	1954-55	Minesweeping Training Squadron, Portsmouth
	1956/67	Operational Reserve Rosneath
	20.12.68	Pounds, Portsmouth for yacht conversion.
	1969	Purchased by Australian Marine for conversion to a ferry boat for use between Adelaide and Port Lincoln.
BUCKLESHAM	1960's	Brought forward from reserve for TRV.
	1960-64	Operational Reserve Rosneath, Land cradled.
	1965	Brought forward from Reserve for T.R.V.
	1978	TRV at Portland.
	1979	For disposal.

Name	Dates	Notes
CARDINHAM	28.7.53	Commissioned at HMS Diligence, Hythe.
	1954/56	232nd M/S.
	1957	Reserve at Rosneath.
	1958	Reserve at Chatham, refit and sheathing.
	1959	Hong Kong RNVR.
	1.4.66	Returned to RN.
	1967	Sold for BU to Wing Luen Hing, Hong Kong.
CHELSHAM	28.7.53	Commissioned at HMS Diligence, Hythe.
	1954/56	232nd M/S.
	1957	Reserve at Rosneath.
	1958	Refit at Portsmouth, sheathing and Preservation.
	1959/60	Reserve at Hythe (land cradled).
	13.12.65	Transferred to RAF at Plymouth as HMFA 5001.
	1971	Returned to RN.
	23.11.73	Sold to Gomba Marine Ltd.
CHILLINGHAM	13.7.53	Commissioned at HMS DILLIGENCE, Hythe
	11.54	Senior Officer 232nd Minesweeping Squadron, Bristol Channel area. Salvage Duties (with ASHELDHAM) in seach for Javelin A/C which crashed near Weston Super Mare.
	1955-56	Refitting at Wivenhoe Shipyard
	1957-58	50th Minesweeping Squadron Port Edgar
	1959-68	Operational Reserve Rosneath, Land cradled.
	5.3.69	Sold to La Societe Maseline Ltd. Sark for yacht conversion
COBHAM	1954/56	232nd M/S.
	1957	Reserve at Sheerness refit and sheathing for service in Far East.
	18.10.58	Sailed from Singapore for Hong Kong with GLENHAM.
	1960	120th M/S Hong Kong.
	5.66	Sold for BU at Singapore.

HMS Cobham (Dec 1955)

HMS Chelsham — mast folded — passes through Teddington Lock en route to Kingston-upon-Thames.

Name	Dates	Notes
CRANHAM	11.54	Agamemnon Boat Yard, Beaulieu for preservation
	1955-60	Operational Reserve, Gosport/Hythe
	1962-63	Operational Reserve Hythe, Land Cradled.
	1966	Sold to W.T. Hunt, Birmingham.
DAMERHAM	1954/55	Operational Reserve, Hythe/Gosport
	1956	Refitting at Whites, Cowes
	1958-62	120th Minesweeping Squadron, Hong Kong
	12.4.62	Arrived Singapore with COBHAM, DARSHAM, GLENTHAM, HOVINGHAM to reduce to reserve
	27.9.66	Sold to Kiaw Aik & Co., Jurong, Singapore for BU.
DARSHAM	1954-55	Operational Reserve, Hythe/Gosport
	1956	Refitting at Chatham
	195-	
	8/1962	120th Minesweeping Squadron Hong Kong.
	1963-64	Operational Reserve, Singapore
	1.4.66	Sold to Kiaw Aik & Co., Jurong, Singapore for BU.
DAVENHAM	1954-55	Operational Reserve, Hythe/Gosport.
	1958/62	120th Minesweeping Squadron Hong Kong.
	1963/64	Operational Reserve Singapore.
	5.66	Sold for BU at Singapore.
DITTISHAM	1955/68	Operational Reserve at Hythe/Gosport
	1968/73	Training Tender for HMS GANGES.
	1973/81	Training Tender for HMS RALEIGH.
	1982	For disposal.
	22.4.83	Towed from Devonport to Dartmouth for further service as Training Ship for Dartmouth Unit Sea Cadet Corps.

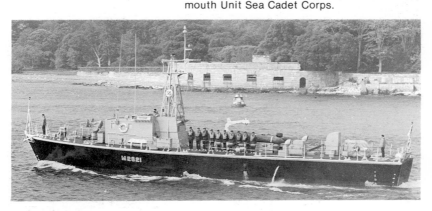

HMS Dittisham

Name	Dates	Notes
DOWNHAM	1956/63	Operational Reserve Rosneath, Land cradled.
	1964/78	T.R.V.
	1979	For disposal.
EDLINGHAM	29.9.56	Extensively damaged by fire at Portsmouth.
	8.5.57	Sold to Pounds for BU.
	1956-64	Operational Reserve Rosneath

Name	Dates	Notes
ELSENHAM	56/64	Operational Reserve Rosneath
	1967	South Yemen Navy.
ETCHINGHAM	1956	Damaged by fire whilst in reserve at Haslar.
	1957/58	Operational Reserve
	1959/65	On loan to Hong Kong R.N.R.
	1.4.66	Returned to RN.
	5.67	BU by Wing Luen Hing, Hong Kong.
EVERINGHAM	1954/64	Operational Reserve Gosport/Hythe
	1964/79	P.A.S./T.R.V.
	1980	Paid off for disposal.

HMS Cranham

Name	Dates	Notes
FELMERSHAM	1954/60	Operational Reserve, Gosport.
	1961/65	Operational Reserve, Singapore.
	5.3.66	Malayan Navy, renamed SRI TOLAK.
FLINTHAM	1955/64	Operational Reserve, Hythe.
	1968/73	Training Tender HMS GANGES.
	1970	Tender to HMS Ganges.
	1974/81	Training Tender HMS RALEIGH.
	8.82	For disposal.
FORDHAM	1957/64	Operational Reserve Rosneath, Land cradled.
	1964	D.G.V.
	1979	For disposal.
	5.81	Sold.

RMAS Fordham after DGV conversion

Name	Dates	Notes
FRETTENHAM	13.12.54	French Navy as TULIPE (M771).
FRITHAM	1954/63	Operational Reserve, Gosport/Hythe.
	1964/78	T.R.V.
	1979	For disposal
GEORGEHAM	1957/65	Operational Reserve Rosneath. Land cradled.
	27.1.68	Sold to Decca Navigator Co. Ltd.
GLENTHAM	18.10.58	Sailed from Singapore in SS BENARTY with COBHAM for Hong Kong and 120th M.S.S.
	1959/62	120th M.S.S. Hong Kong.
	3.63	Reducing to Reserve at Singapore
	1.4.66	Sold to Kiaw Aik & Co., Jurong, Singapore for BU.

The large & the small . . . HMS Glentham steams past ships of the USN at Hong Kong

Name	Dates	Notes
GREETHAM	1955/61	Operational Reserve Gosport
	11.62	With HARPHAM sailed for Libya as ZUARA
HALSHAM	1955/63	Operational Reserve, Gosport/Hythe.
	1964	For Disposal.
	1966	To R.A.F. as HMFA 5002
	1974	To Royal Corps of Transport as R.G. MASTERS V.C.
HARPHAM	1955-1962	Operational Reserve, Gosport/Hythe.
	11.62	With GREETHAM sailed for Libya as BRAK.
HAVERSHAM	1954/63	Operational Reserve, Gosport/Hythe.
	1964/79	T.R.V.
	1980	Paid off.
HILDERSHAM	1955	Transferred to Indian Navy renamed BIMLIPITAN (M2705).
HOVINGHAM	1956/57	Operational Reserve, Hythe/Rosneath.
	1958/62	120th M.S.S. Hong Kong.
	1963/64	Operational Reserve Singapore.
	27.9.66	Sold to Kiaw Aik & Co., Jurong, Singapore for BU.
INGLESHAM	1954/58	50th M.S.S., Port Edgar.
	1959/63	Operational Reserve Hythe.
	29.9.66	Sold to A.F. Van Riel, Antwerp for BU at Rotterdam.

First of the class . . . HMS Inglesham on builders sea trials.

Name	Dates	Notes
ISHAM	1955	NATO — French OEILLET (M774).
KINGHAM	1955	NATO — French PAQUERETTE (775).
LASHAM	1955/57	Operational Reserve, Gosport
	1958/63	Operational Reserve, Hythe.
	1964/79	T.R.V.
	9.81	Sold.
LEDSHAM	1955/56	Senior Officer, 232nd M.S.S.
	1957/65	Operational Reserve, Rosneath, Land Cradled.
	1967	Clyde Division RNR as accommodation ship.
	21.4.71	Sold to Metal recoveries (Newhaven) for BU.
LITTLESHAM	1955	Transferred to Indian Navy renamed BASSEIN.

Name	Dates	Notes
LUDHAM	1955/56	232nd M/S.
	1957	Sheerness refit sheathing and Preservation.
	1958/60	Rosneath reserve (Land Cradled).
	13.3.67	Sold to Oceanographic Section, Strathclyde University.
MALHAM	2.10.59	To Ghana renamed YOGODA (M11).
MERSHAM	1955	Transferred to France under the U.S. 'off shore' procurement programme, renamed VIOLETTE (M.773).
MICKLEHAM	1955/64	Operational Reserve. Hythe. Land Cradled.
	1965	For Disposal.
	29.9.66	Sold to Gaston Builders Ltd., Wraysbury, Bucks., for conversion.
MILEHAM	1955	Transferred to French Navy as 'HORTENSIA' (M.783).
NEASHAM	1957/67	Operational Reserve, Rosneath, Land Cradled.
	1968	Transferred to Australia. Renamed 'TORTOISE'—Diving Tender at Sydney.
NETTLEHAM	1957/65	Operational Reserve, Rosneath, Land Cradled.
	1966	Disposal List approved to Scrap.
	19.1.68	Sold to Rye A.R.C. Ltd., London for conversion to repair boat on the Thames.
OCKHAM	1956/66	Operational Reserve, Hythe, Land Cradled.
	12.9.67	Sold to Belcon Shipping & Trading, London for conversion to yacht.
ODIHAM	1956/63	Operational Reserve, Rosneath, Land Cradled.
	1964/78	R.N.X.S.
	1979	Disposal List
	5.80	Sold to Sutton & Smith, Ltd., Great Wakering, Essex.
OTTRINGHAM	31.10.59	Sailed for Ghana.
	11.59	Officially transferred from R.N. to Ghana at Takoradi and renamed 'AFADZATO'.
PAGHAM	1956/63	Operational Reserve, Rosneath, Land Cradled.
	1964/74	R.N.X.S.
	1982/83	R.N.R. Tender.
PETERSHAM	1955	Transferred to France under the U.S. 'Off shore' procurement programme. Renamed 'CAPUCINE' (M.782).
PINEHAM	10.11.55	Handed over to France at Hythe. Renamed 'PETUNIA' (M.789).
POLSHAM	1958/66	Operational Reserve, Hythe.
	23.2.67	Sold to Port of London Authority for Hydrographic duties, renamed 'MAPLIN'.
POPHAM	1955/56	Operational Reserve Hythe.
	1957/63	Operational Reserve Rosneath, Land Cradled.
	9.6.66	Transferred to Australian Navy, renamed 'SEAL' (Y.298).
PORTISHAM	1956/63	Operational Reserve, Rosneath, Land Cradled.
	1964/83	R.N.X.S. Portsmouth.

Name	Dates	Notes
POWDERHAM	1958	Operational Reserve, Hythe.
	11.59	Special Trials.
	1960	Operational Reserve, Hythe.
	1961/62	Forth Division R.N.R.
	3.63	Portsmouth for Special Trials.
	1964	Converted to Inshore Survey Craft renamed WATERWITCH.
	8.82	Liverpool University R.N. Unit Tender.
PULHAM	1956	London R.N.R. as 'ISIS'.
	1963	Reverted to 'PULHAM'.
	29.9.66	Sold to A.E. Pierce & Sons, Canvey Island.

RNXS Portisham — all minesweeping gear removed

Name	Dates	Notes
PUTTENHAM	1958/63	Operational Reserve, Rosneath, Land Cradled.
	1964/78	R.N.X.S. Plymouth.
	1980	Sold.
RACKHAM	8.56	Operational Reserve, Hythe.
	11.56-63	Operational Reserve, Rosneath, Land Cradled.
	1964	Brought forward from Reserve for R.N.X.S.
	1966	Disposal list.
RAMPISHAM	11.57	Operational Reserve Hythe.
	1958/59	3rd Division F.P.S. renamed SQUIRREL.
	1960/63	Operational Reserve, Hythe.
	29.9.66	Sold to A.E. Pierce & Sons, Canvey Is. for BU at Pitsea.
REEDHAM	1959	50th M.S.S. Portland having replaced CHILLINGHAM.
	11.60	At Greenock, attached to Clyde R.N.R.
	1961/62	Refit at Chatham.
	1962/63	Operational Reserve Hythe.
	29.9.66	Sold to Pounds.

HMS Reedham (July 1959)

Name	Dates	Notes
RENDLESHAM	1955	Transferred to French Navy—renamed 'AUBEPINE' (M.781).
RIPLINGHAM	1955	Transferred to French Navy—renamed 'MYOSOTIS' (M.788).
SANDRINGHAM	11.57	Operational Reserve, Gosport.
	1958/65	Operational Reserve, Rosneath, Land Cradled.
	1966	Disposal List.
	1972/83	Personnel Transport Clyde area.

HMS Sandringham — before conversion

Name	Dates	Notes
SAXLINGHAM	1957/63	Operational Reserve, Rosneath, Land Cradled.
	1964/65	R.N.X.S.
	1966	Approved to scrap.
	2.5.68	Sold to Ross & Cromarty CC for use as a tender for Lewis Sea School.
SHIPHAM	1956/64	Operational Reserve Rosneath Land Cradled.
	1964/83	R.N.X.S. Meadway.
SHIPPINGHAM	1955	To France. Renamed 'DAHLIA' (M.786).
SHRIVENHAM	1956/63	Operational Reserve, Rosneath, Land cradled.
	1964/65	R.N.X.S.
	1966	For Disposal.
	21.2.69	Sold to Port of London Authority.
SIDLESHAM	1956/7	Operational Reserve Hythe/Gosport.
	1958/63	Operational Reserve Rosneath, Land cradled.
	1964	Disposal List. Sold to Sussex Constabulary as H.Q. for Sailing Club.

HMS Sidlesham

Name	Dates	Notes
SPARHAM	1955	To France. Renamed 'HIBISCUS' (M.785).
STEDHAM	1955	To France. Renamed 'JASMIN' (M.766).
SULHAM	1955	To France. Renamed 'JONQUILLE' (M.787).
THAKEHAM	1958/63	Operational Reserve Rosneath, Land Cradled.
	1964/78	R.N.X.S.
	1979	For Disposal.
THATCHAM	1958/70	Operational Reserve.
	1971/78	D.G.V.
	1979	For Disposal.
	1982/83	R.N.R. Tender.
THORNHAM	1958/65	Operational Reserve
	1966	For Disposal.
	1972-81	Aberdeen University RN Unit.
	9.6.81	Damaged when a mobile crane crashed onto her deck at Aberdeen.
	1.84	Laid up at Rosyth.
TIBENHAM	1955	To France. Renamed 'GERANIUM' (M.784).
TONGHAM	1958/63	Operational Reserve Rosneath.
	1964/78	R.N.X.S./P.A.S.
	1979	For Disposal.
TRESHAM	1956/63	Operational Reserve Hythe.
	2.64	For Disposal.
	8.4.68	Handed over to Reardon Smith Nautical College, Cardiff renamed 'MARGHERITA'.
WARMINGHAM	1957/69	Operational Reserve Rosneath. Land cradled.
	1970/80	D.G.V.
	1981	For Disposal.
WEXHAM	1955	To France. Renamed 'ARMOISE' (M.772).
WINTRINGHAM	1957/63	Operational Reserve Rosneath.
	2.64	For Disposal.
	9.6.66	To Australia. Renamed 'OTTER' (Y.299). Converted to Diving Tender, Sydney.
WOLDINGHAM	1957/64	Operational Reserve Rosneath.
	1964	Brought forward from Reserve for R.N.X.S.
	29.9.66	Sold to Pounds of Portsmouth.
WRENTHAM	1956	Operational Reserve, Gosport.
	1958/63	Operational Reserve Hythe.
	1966	Sold to Divcon International U.K. Ltd., for conversion as Diving Service Vessel—North Sea.
YAXHAM	1959/62	50th M.S.S. Portland.
	1962/63	3rd M.S.S.
	1964	Conversion to Inshore Survey Craft, renamed 'WOODLARK'.

HMS Woodlark (Ex. Yaxham)

The Great Fire . . . Blazing Inshore Minesweepers at their lay-up berths in Haslar Creek at Gosport. They were later towed, on fire, into mid harbour to prevent the blaze spreading. 24 Sept. 1956.

INSHORE MINEHUNTERS — LEY CLASS

Displacement:	123 tons (standard) 164 (full load).
Dimensions:	100 (pp) 106 5/6 (oa) x 21⅔ x 15½ '
Guns:	1 - 40mm Bofors A.A. or 1 - 20mm Oerlikon AA
Machinery:	2 Paxman Diesels BHP 550 = 14 knots. (9 kts sweeping).
Oil Fuel:	15 tons.
Complement:	15 (Peace) 22 (War).

The 'Ley' class differed from the 'Ham' class. They were of composite (non-magnetic metal and wooden) construction, instead of all wooden construction. They had no winch or sweeping gear, as they were mine hunters not sweepers. They had smaller engines as less towing power was required.

Name	PT No	Completion Date	Builders
AVELEY	M.2002	3. 2.54	J. Samuel White
BREARLEY	M.2003	15. 4.55	J. Samuel White
BRENCHLEY	M.2004	22. 9.54	Saunders Roe
BRINKLEY	M.2005	3.11.54	Saunders Roe
BROADLEY	M.2006	12. 9.54	Blackmore
BROOMLEY	M.2007	5. 8.54	P.K. Harris
BURLEY	M.2008	29. 6.54	Dorset Yacht Co.
CHAILEY	M.2009	7. 1.55	Saunders Roe
CRADLEY	M.2010	5. 5.55	Saunders Roe
DINGLEY	M.2001	22. 7.54	J. Samuel White

HMS Aveley as completed

Name	Dates	Notes
AVELEY	1954/56	51st M/S Port Edgar.
	1957	Reserve at Rosneath.
	1958	Rosneath (Land Cradled).
	1963/80	Training Tender at Plymouth.
	1982	For disposal.
	1983	Woolwich Sea Cadet Corps.
BREARLEY	1955/56	Reserve at HMS Hornet, Gosport.
	1957	50th M/S Port Edgar.
	1960	51st M/S.
	1963	Dartmouth Training Tender.
	1969	Disposal List.
	1.73	Pounds Portsmouth for BU

HMS Brearley

BRENCHLEY	1954/60	51st M/S.
	1.10.62	1st Minehunter Squadron
	1965	Disposal List.
	1966	Sold.
BRINKLEY	1954/56	51st M/S.
	1956/60	50th M/S.
	3.60	51st M/S.
	1.10.62	1st Minehunter Squadron.
	1965	Disposal List.
	1966	Sold for BU.
BROADLEY	1954	J. White Cowes, for Preservation.
	1955/56	Reserve HMS Hornet, Gosport.
	28.9.56	Extensively damaged by fire at HMS Hornet.
	6.11.56	Portsmouth for docking.
	1957	Reserve.
	1959	Scapped.

Name	Dates	Notes
BROOMLEY	1954	Dorset Yacht Company Poole for preservation.
	1955/57	Reserve at HMS Hornet.
	1958	Docking and fitting out at Portsmouth for Fishery Protection Squadron.
	1.59	Renamed WATCHFUL. 3rd Division FPS based at Portland.
	1966	For disposal.
	21.3.68	Arrived Rotterdam for BU.

HMS Broomley

Name	Dates	Notes
BURLEY	1955/56	50th M/S Port Edgar.
	1957	51st M/S Port Edgar.
	1.60	Fishery Protection Squadron vice RAMPISHAM (SQUIRREL) 3rd Division Channel.
	21.3.68	Arrived Rotterdam with BROOMLEY for BU.
CHAILEY	1955/60	51st M/S.
	1965	Sales List.
	1969	Sold for BU.
CRADLEY	1955	Vospers, Porchester for preservation.
	1956/58	Operational reserve
	1959	Reserve Hythe (Land Cradled).
	1963	Allocated to London Division RNR renamed ISIS.
	1974/81	Affiliated to Southampton University RN Unit.

HMS Cradley (as Isis)

Name	Dates	Notes
DINGLEY	1954/60	Home Station Clearance Diving Team Tender.
	1967	For disposal.
	1968	Sold to Pounds, Portsmouth.

HMS Dingley

HUNT CLASS MCMV's

Displacement:	625 tonnes.
Dimensions:	60m x 10m x 2.9m
Main Engines:	2 Ruston-Paxman 9-59K Deltic diesels; 1,900 bhp = 16 knots. Three 200 kw diesel generators. Pulse Generator. (Fitted with hydraulic drive for slow running up to 8 knots).
Range—Miles:	1500 at 12 knots.
Sensors and Armament:	Plessey 193 M Minehunting sonar. Decca QM14 and Hi Fix. CAAIS system. Two PAP mine disposal vehicles. Double Oropesa Wire sweep. Magnetic sweep, Acoustic sweep. One 40 mm Bofors gun.
Complement:	45 (6 officers, 39 ratings).

HMS Brecon returns from the Falklands

Name	PT. No.	Launched	Accepted	Builders
BRECON	M.29	21.6.78	6.12.79	Vosper Thornycroft, Southampton
LEDBURY	M.30	5.12.79	18.3.81	Vosper Thornycroft, Southampton
CATTISTOCK	M.31	21.1.81	5.3.82	Vosper Thornycroft, Southampton
COTTESMORE	M.32	9.2.82	3.83	Yarrow, Scotstoun
BROCKLESBY	M.33	12.1.82	25.10.82	Vosper Thornycroft, Southampton
MIDDLETON	M.34	27.4.83		Yarrow, Scotstoun
DULVERTON	M.35	3.11.82	5.10.83	Vosper Thornycroft, Southampton
CHIDDINGFOLD	M.37	6.10.83		Vosper Thornycroft, Southampton
ATHERSTONE	M.38	Building		Vosper Thornycroft, Southampton
BICESTER	M.36	Building		Vosper Thornycroft, Southampton
HURWORTH	M.39	Building		Vosper Thornycroft, Southampton

Name	Dates	Notes
BRECON	6.12.79	Handed over to R.N. at H.M.S. VERNON for 1st MCMS (Rosyth)
	8.82	Arrived Port Stanley, Falkland Island.
	15.9.82	Arrived Rosyth (with Ledbury) from Falkland Islands on completion of a five week patrol which included the clearing of two Argentine minefields, Ordnance clearance of San Carlos water, Port San Carlos and Fox Bay. She also carried out wreck location and route survey.
BROCKLESBY	9.8.82	Arrived Portsmouth from trials.
	25.10.82	Handed over to R.N. at Portsmouth
	2.83	Commissioned at Portsmouth — 1st M.C.M.S.
	24.2.83	Damaged in collision with 'NURTON' off Portland in thick fog — slight bow damage.
CATTISTOCK	5.3.82	Handed over to R.N. at Portsmouth.
	16.6.82	Commissioned at H.M.S. VERNON for 1st M.C.M.S.
LEDBURY	18.3.81	Accepted by R.N. at Portsmouth.
	11.6.81	Commissioned for 1st M.C.M.S.
	15.9.82	See Brecon
	9.83	Major fire onboard — towed to Zeebrugge.
COTTESMORE	1983	1st MCMS

HMS Cottesmore

HMS Ledbury

11th MINE COUNTERMEASURES SQUADRON

Name	Displacement	Launched	Completed	Builders
CORDELLA	1,238 tons	2.73	5.73	Clelands Shipbuilding Co Ltd., Wallsend
FARNELLA	1,207 tons	2.12.71	4.72	Clelands Shipbuilding Co. Ltd., Wallsend
JUNELLA	1,615 tons	9.9.75	12.75	Clelands Shipbuilding Co. Ltd., Wallsend
NORTHELLA	1,238 tons	7.73	11.73	Clelands Shipbuilding Co. Ltd., Wallsend
PICT	1,478 tons	-	-	Brooke Marine Ltd., Lowestoft

Dimensions:-		
CORDELLA, FARNELLA and NORTHELLA	70.20m x 12.70m x 8.11m
JUNELLA	66.25m x 13.14m x 8.11m
PICT	70.11m x 8.39m

During April, 1982, CORDELLA, FARNELLA, JUNELLA and NORTHELLA former Stern Trawlers were requisitioned from their owners, J. Marr & Son, Ltd., of Hull, whilst PICT was requisitioned from British United Trawlers Finance Ltd., Hull.

They were fitted out as minesweepers at Rosyth and formed the 11th MCM Squadron for duty in the South Atlantic. Their ship's companies were formed mainly of men from the 1st MCM and Fishery Protection Squadrons.

Operating in the South Atlantic, the 11th MCM Squadron carried out the transfer of 3,000 troops and their equipment from the QUEEN ELIZABETH II to the CANBERRA at South Georgia. They were also involved in many night landings of S.A.S. and S.B.S. units on the Falklands.

H.M.S. PICT was the first vessel to enter Port Stanley after the surrender.

During minesweeping operations PICT landed most of her ship's company ashore, the danger of being sunk was considered high—due to the large number of mines located. She was manned by a crew of 14—the minimum considered necessary.

JUNELLA one of the five which returned to Rosyth from the Falklands on 11th August, 1982, brought back over her stern a large green mine—defused, but still packed with enough explosive to sink a ship. She had acted as mine disposal ship outside Port Stanley and a "Sample" was required at home.

After de-commissioning at Rosyth the trawlers returned to the Humber to be refitted in civilian yards, and during October/November, 1982, were returned to their owners.

NORTHELLA was once again chartered by MOD (N) in 1983 for duties in the Clyde approaches, but not in a minesweeping role.

The 11th MCM Squadron return from the Falkland Islands 11 August 1982.

RIVER CLASS

Displacement: 850 tons approx.

Dimensions: 47.0m (oa) x 10.5m x 3.1m (deep draught)

Propulsion: Twin Shaft - 4 bladed CP propellers
2 Ruston 6 RKC diesel engines, each developing 1520 BHP
(1130Kw) at 900 rpm. Speed 13 knots.

Complement: 30 — 7 Officers, 23 Ratings

Name	Pt. No.	Builders	Completed
BLACKWATER	M.2008	Richards, Yarmouth	Building.
CARRON	M.2004	Richards, Yarmouth	1984.
DOVEY	M.2005	Richards, Yarmouth	1984.
HELFORD	M.2006	Richards, Yarmouth	Building.
HELMSDALE	M.2010	Richards, Lowestoft	Building.
HUMBER	M.2007	Richards, Lowestoft	Building.
ITCHEN	M.2009	Richards, Lowestoft	Building.
WAVENEY	M.2003	Richards, Lowestoft	1984.

Note

A new class of Minesweeper entering service with the Royal Naval Reserve.

HMS Waveney

The Shape of Minesweepers to come . . .

Displacement   450 tons
Dimensions   50m x 9m
Machinery   Twin Vectored thrust units
Complement   40

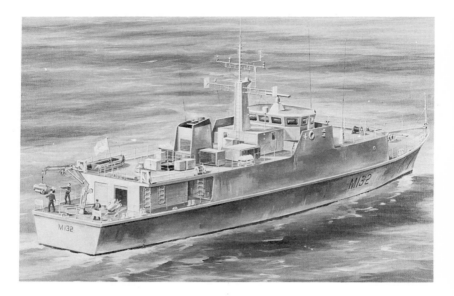

The Ministry of Defence has approved the design for the new Single Role Minehunter that Vosper Thornycroft (UK) Ltd have developed.

The design is an entirely new concept of a Single Role Minehunter, a simple, low cost, but effective vessel for detecting, classifying and destroying mines.

The new ships, which will replace some of the old Ton-class will be built in Glass Reinforced Plastic—chosen for its non-magnetic signature, strength and shock resistance. It does not corrode, rot, warp, shrink or split and is resistant to marine borers. It is easy to maintain and simple and quick to repair. The main hull is designed on the basis of minimum cost. The advances made in this design over previous minehunters relate to low cost and weight and particularly higher shock resistance, which meet the latest NATO requirements.

The accommodation spaces for 7 officers and 33 ratings have been arranged in the centre section of the ship in order to improve sea-going habitability and reduce crew fatigue—both by the reduction of motion and ambient noise. The main operations spaces are also sited centrally.

Machinery consists of twin, low magnetic, diesel engines each driving one of the Vectored Thrust Units. 3 diesel generators are fitted. For quiet operation whilst minehunting the thrust units are driven by electric motors. A fully integrated variable depth sonar and a remote control mine disposal system, along with facilities for divers, are fitted. One small calibre gun is included for self defence.

MINESWEEPER DEPOT & SUPPORT SHIPS

HMS Narvik (1960) Depot ship to the 108th Minesweeping Squadron (& local Submarine Squadron)—Msida Creek Malta.

'WOODBRIDGE HAVEN'
(ex Loch Torridon)

Builders:	Swan Hunter & Wigham Richardson, Wallsend.
Launched:	13.1.1945.
Displacement:	1,652 tons.
Dimensions:	307' 4" x 38'6" x 12'9".
Speed:	19.5 knots.
Armament:	1 - 4"m 6 - 20 mm AA.
Complement:	103.

Originally constructed as a frigate but converted to a submarine Depot Ship and later as Headquarters ship for coastal minesweepers.

1946 - 1954	Used as Target ship 3rd S/M Flotilla Rothesay.
1955	Commissioned as Headquarters ship of 2nd Minesweeping Squadron.
1957	Captain Minesweepers, Mediterranean.
1958-60	Captain Inshore Flotilla, Mediterranean.
1960-63	Captain Inshore Flotilla, Far East.
1963	Paid Off.
9.8.65	Left Portsmouth in tow for Blyth to be broken up.

HMS Woodbridge Haven

HMS Mull of Kintyre

'MULL OF GALLOWAY'
(ex Kinnard Head)

Builders:	North Vancouver Ship Repairs Ltd.
Launched:	26.10.44
Displacement:	8,500 tons.
Dimensions:	441'6" x 57'6" x 20'3".
Speed:	11 knots.
Armament:	16 - 20 mm.

1947	In Reserve.
1947 - 1949	Headquarters Ship of Senior Officer Reserve Fleet, Clyde.
1950	Paid Off.
1954	Re-commissioned to become Inshore Minesweeping Flotilla Headquarters Ship.
1957	In Reserve.
16.2.65	Left Portsmouth in tow bound for Hamburg to be broken up.

'MULL OF KINTYRE'

Builders:	North Vancouver Ship Repairs Ltd.
Launched:	5.4.45.

1950	Paid Off.
1955	Brought forward as Armament Maintainance Ship, but later became Repair and Accommodation Ship.
8.61	Completed conversion to Minesweeper Maintainance Ship for service at Singapore.
12.69	Sold to Hong Kong Shipbreakers. She broke away from her tow on 19.12.69 but was re-covered and towed to Manilla.

H.M.S. MANXMAN

Builder:	Stephen & Son.
Launched:	5.9.40.
Displacement:	2,650 tons (4,000 tons full load).
Dimensions:	418' (oa) x 40' x 11'
Guns:	6 - 4" 6 - 40 mm AA.
Mines:	100.
Machinery:	Parsons geared turbines, 2 shafts SHP 72,000 = 40 knots max. (Reduced to 26 knots when converted).

In April, 1945, 'MANXMAN' was recommissioned for service with the British Pacific Fleet after undergoing repairs to war damage. She did not however, arrive at Colombo until 14th July, and at the time of the Japanese capitulation, a month later, was at Melbourne. She remained with the British Pacific Fleet until June, 1946, and after a refit at Chatham returned again to the Far East from February to December, 1947, after which she returned home and paid off into reserve.

'MANXMAN' was recommissioned in 1951 for service in the Mediterranean.

In March, 1956 she left Malta with stores for relief of the victims of the earthquake in the Lebanon and after unloading at Beirut, sailed for Port Said to refuel before returning to Malta. She took part in the Suez Operations in November, 1956, and continued in the Mediterranean until 1957, when she was placed in reserve.

In 1960 she was taken in hand for conversion into a Minesweeping Support Ship by Chatham Dockyard. The conversion took over two years—airconditioning for service in the Far East was installed and the virtual rebuilding of her interior to take the extra auxiliary machinery and store rooms required for her new rôle was necessary.

On completion of the conversion in 1963 H.M.S. 'MANXMAN' sailed for the Far East where she relieved H.M.S. 'WOODBRIDGE HAVEN' as Forward Support Ship for the Inshore Flotilla (Far East).

She returned to Portsmouth on 19th December, 1968, and commissioned the following year as an Engineer Officers training ship.

'MANXMAN' arrived at Newport on 6.10.72 for breaking up by J. Cashmore Ltd.

H.M.S. ABDIEL

HMS ABDIEL (with MAXTON & WILTON alongside) during the clearance of the Suez Canal (1974).

Builder:	Vosper Thornycroft (Southampton).
Length:	264'.
Beam:	38½'.
Draught (full load)	9'3".
Displacement (full load)	1460 tons.
Speed	16 knots.
Completed:	17.10.67.

Designed to act in support of mine countermeasures craft the 'ABDIEL' is a multi-purpose vessel. In addition to her workshop facilities she also has provision for the headquarters staff that would be required in a large-scale mine warfare operation. She can both lay and recover exercise minefields for the practical training of M.C.M. vessels.

A variety of other HM Ships have spent part of their career as "Depot ships" for minesweepers. They include HM Ships Reclaim, Hartland Point, Plover & RFA Sea Salvor.

The Forgotten Fleet—at Hythe (Southampton Water)

Coastal Minesweepers spent many years laid up in Reserve—in ports worldwide. They normally had wooden/asbestos "sheds" built over them to protect equipment & decking.

End of the Road . . .

HMS ESPIEGLE—Heads for the scrapyard at Dalmuir.

HMS Quainton—a sorry sight as the shipbreakers tear her apart (Nov 1979).

INDEX

Abbreviations

AA .... Anti Aircraft
AC .... Aircraft.
A/S .... Anti-Submarine.
BU .... Broken Up.
BYMS .... British Yard
Minesweeper.
DCT .... Depth Charge Thrower.
DGV .... Degaussing Vessel.
FOCBNG ..... Flag Officer British
Naval Forces Germany
FPS .... Fishery Protection
Squadron.
HMAS .... Her Majesty's
Australian Ship.
GRP .... Glass Reinforced
Plastic.
HQ .... Headquarters.
LL .... The main magnetic
sweep, consisting of a
pair of insulated and
buoyant electric
cables towed astern of
the minesweeper,
activated by a
generator or batteries.
MCMS .... Mine
Countermeasures
Squadron.

MMS .... Motor Minesweeper.
M/S .... Minesweeper.
MSS .... Minesweeping
Squadron.
OROPESA .... Sweep. The name for
the standard sweep
wire (named after an
RN trawler in which
the sweep was first
developed in 1919).
(oa) .... Overall length.
(pp) .... Perpendicular length.
(qv) .... see.
RNR .... Royal Naval Reserve.
RNVR .... Royal Naval Volunteer
Reserve.
RNXS .... Royal Naval Auxiliary
Service.
S.O. .... Senior Officer.
SORF .... Senior Officer Reserve
Fleet.
STANAV-
FORCHAN ... Standing Naval Force
Channel. (NATO)
TRV .... Torpedo Recovery
Vessel.
USN .... United States Navy.